Away, Tangled Past

To the Future Through Poland and Germany

For my friend
Vivian Jones
with abiding
affection —

Yours,

Sam Pisar

June 6, 2013

Away, Tangled Past

To the Future Through Poland and Germany

JANE PEJSA

Edited and Composed by Barbara Field
Cover Designed by Justine Pawelski
Printed by Worzalla Publishing Company
Stevens Point, Wisconsin

Kenwood Publishing
1314 Marquette Avenue, Suite1206
Minneapolis, Minnesota 55403-4146
(612) 354-3411

Cataloging-in-Publication Data
Pejsa, Jane, 1929–
    Away, Tangled Past: To the Future Through Poland and Germany.
    Includes bibliography, index.
    1. World War II—History. 2. Holocaust. 3. Poland.
4. Germany. 5. Pomorze/Pommern. 6. Dresden. 7. Berlin.
8. Naziism. 9. Communism. 10. Free Poland. 11. United
Germany.

iv

For
Michael Ripke and
Katrina Ripke Söderberg-Jahn
in memory of
their mother
Raba Stahlberg Ripke-Heckscher

Contents

Illustrations	ix
Preface	xi
Acknowledgments	xv
Prologue	1

Pomorze in Poland

1. Gateway to Poland	5
2. Heart of Kleistland	11

Kozalin—Tutaj, Here, Hier

3. Metamorphosis	29
4. The Discovery	37

Dresden in Saxony

5. A Word About Saxony	49
6. The Nazi Times	51
7. The Klemperer Diaries	55
8. The Final Solution	62
9. The Destruction of Dresden	66
10. Return of the Natives	72

Dresden Resurrected

11. How It All Happened	81
12. Die Wende (The Change)	96
13. Ahead of the Curve	109

CONTENTS

Berlin Beyond the Crossing

14. Mitte 117
15. Weimar 120
16. *Götterdämmerung* 124
17. Postscript to the Twentieth Century 130
18. Berlin in the Twenty-first Century 133

Epilogue 143
Bibliography 145
Index of Names 147

Illustrations

Artist's Rendering of *Das Kugelhaus*   Cover Illustration*

Stalag Luft IV, POW Memorial   10

World War I Memorial Oak Grove   19

Kikowo Pałac, a work in progress   22

On the right, Robert, Peter Zimmerling, and Jane among a
bevy of students from the Leipzig University   22

Bursztynowy Pałac (The Amber Hotel)   32

Glimpse of the hotel gardens   32

Ks. Henryk Romanik with the foursome viewing the resurrected
"F. Marx" and "David Baruch" burial stones at the Old Jewish
Cemetery   42

Zdzisław Pacholski (Zibi) with Henryk at the plaque
commemorating the destruction of the Koszalin synagogue,
Kristallnacht 1938   42

Evening in the bar of the Amber Hotel   45

Dresden postcard 1935: Semper Opera House, Bellevue Hotel,
Elbe River   52

Three Americans dwarfed by the gate inside the Zwinger   108

*Designed by Justine Pawelski, justinpaw@g2a.net.

ILLUSTRATIONS

Saturday evening, Bach's B minor Mass in concert at the
Frauenkirche 108

Auto of the future, at the VW Transparent Factory 112

Success at the Boxhagenerplatz flea market 134

Katrina Söderberg-Jahn, with Helen, at the Park Inn Hotel 134

The Reichstag Transparent Dome, from the Spree River 138

Calling on Karl Marx and Friedrich Engels 138

Keeping pace with Dresden's transparent VW assembly plant
and the Reichstag's transparent dome, the Park Inn guest rooms
now have transparent baths. 140

Photos courtesy Helen Kuehn, Zdzisław Pacholski, and Michael Ripke.

Preface

How did this tale of a tangled past begin? One might reply, it was just one thing after the other.

Perhaps the first awareness dawned on a trip to Berlin in 1956, a time when the newly democratic West Berlin was surrounded by Greater East Berlin, hardly a democratic stronghold. More than a decade after the final Battle for Berlin, bathtubs were still dangling high up from copper pipes on multifamily buildings, their facades long ago removed as rubble. This was West Berlin. Interesting, thought I. Really more interesting than rubble-free West Germany, with a population busy rebuilding, thanks to hard work, good organization, and plenty of American Marshall Plan dollars.

Amost two decades later—a sea voyage to Central Europe by way of Trieste in Italy. Here the highlight was Dresden, that magnificent baroque city destroyed by American and British bombers in World War II. As the years marched on, the destruction of this one city seemed to bring more tears than the millions upon millions of lives lost across the European continent. In fact one of Germany's great twentieth-century poets Erich Kästner, a native of Dresden, was moved to write:

> In a thousand years was her beauty built, in one night was it utterly destroyed.

In the year I first visited Dresden, the poet was more than half right. I was greeted by plenty of cleaned-up empty areas all across the city and a single reconstructed baroque beauty in the Old City.

A decade later, 1986, my first visit to Pomorze in Poland, land of those great Soviet-style state farms that never delivered what they promised. A generation earlier this had been Hinterpommern in Germany. Over several centuries, Pommern was the heart of Germany's landed aristocracy. The estates were large, the life and livelihood of entire villages depending on the landowner and a good crop. He, or she, ruled from the manor house, for which the German word *Der Schloss* translates as "the castle."

This seemingly obscure destination evolved through my interest in the life and death of a twentieth-century German theologian. He had stood against the Nazis and for this was executed shortly before the end of World War II. His name was Dietrich Bonhoeffer, and I intended to write a book about him. And what had this to do with my destination, Pomorze? Oddly enough in this land of the German Junkers once lived families who staunchly opposed the Nazi message and later the events leading to persecution of Jews, Slavs, whatever, ultimately to war, the Holocaust, and finally for Germany a disaster of horrendous proportions.

The family Kleist of Kieckow in Pommern, especially the matriarch herself, supported and underwrote much of Bonhoeffer's efforts to stop the tide before it engulfed them all, which eventually it did.

After that it continued to be just one thing after another. The lands belonging to the family Kleist in Kieckow in Pommern became the State Farm Kikowo in Pomorze, a tiny, tiny piece of all that happened beginning in 1944 and not trailing off until 1950. During those six years some twelve to fourteen million ethnic Germans either fled or more likely were expelled from their homelands east of the Oder and Neisse rivers. These lands had become part of Poland, Czechoslovakia, and Russia. Some might see it as a simple redrawing of national borders following a punishing war. In those years there were names for these millions—refugees, displaced persons, victims of ethnic cleansing and genocide. And there were other nationalities also—out of Russia, Hungary, Lithuania, Ukraine—many with horrifying tales to tell and each forced to seek a new homeland.

Fast forward to 1989. It would sorely belittle what happened that year to suggest it was just one more thing after the other that brought down the Berlin Wall, melted the iron curtain, and led to the reunification of East and West Germany. It was transformative in the best sense. At that time we were just publishing my book *Matriarch of Conspiracy, Ruth von Kleist 1867-1945*. This was the tale of the Kleists of Kieckow with a good bit of Dietrich Bonhoeffer thrown in, bringing to life cataclysmic events of the previous half-century. The book garnered several prizes.

Why not visit the places of the Kleist tale and meet the people who now dwell on these lands? And so we did, first with a few friends, placing plasticized posters marking sites related to Dietrich Bonhoeffer's last years of freedom. That was in 1996. We published a small book—*To Pomerania in Search of Dietrich Bonhoeffer*. Garnering additional interest, particularly when factoring in Bonhoeffer's reaction to events of *Kristallnacht* 1938, we planned another trip. Now with twenty travelers, we returned to Pomorze and mounted six permanent memorial plaques—three Bonhoeffer sites, two sites of destroyed synagogues, and a destroyed Jewish cemetery. Again we published a book—*To Pomerania Where Bonhoeffer Met the Holocaust.*

More than two decades later three veterans of these earlier forays felt a longing to connect back to Poland and Germany. We suspected mighty changes had taken place in the meantime. We were not disappointed. It was not so much the brick and stone, nor even the gait and dress of the people, rather a transformation in attitudes. We discovered a broadening sense of community—a growing together from both sides of the Oder and Neisse rivers. In both Poland and Germany we could almost taste the words—Away, Tangled Past!

Minneapolis   JANE PEJSA
September 2012

Acknowledgments

First of all, I acknowledge with gratitude my adventuresome friends Helen Kuehn and Robert Vockrodt, who joined me on this revisit to Poland, Dresden, and Berlin, not knowing exactly what we might experience along the way. A whole new level of exploration was added when our friends Michael Ripke of Heidelberg and his sister Katrina Söderberg-Jahn of Hannover also signed on. Michael came with his Swedish Volvo, which transformed any ordinariness along the way into a magical experience.

Within the tale I have cited the many other friends and acquaintances who together transformed this sojourn through parts of Poland and Germany into a magic carpet experience. To each one let me now express my joy and my gratitude.

Over the years I have been blessed with friends and acquaintances who were willing to read a manuscript that leads from an ordinary trip in a Volvo automobile into and out of some extraordinary European history, much of it quite personal. The first readers were my two American pals, plus Michael and Katrina, all of whom had suggestions—even corrections—of one kind or another. Thank you all, dear fellow travelers.

Likewise to Jim Lenfesty who interrupted his own literary work to review the draft manuscript, promptly recognizing the direction it was taking. Thus did he guide me away from meaningless titles that taken alone might have been all too clever. Thank you, Jim.

Besides these good friends, others have also reviewed the entire manuscript, or key parts of it: Lisa Reed of Minnesota; Theresa Wanta of Wisconsin; Leslie Brent of London, UK; Zdzisław Pacholski and Ks. Henryk Romanik of Poland; Gerhard Rühlow, Martin Hüneke, and Gerd Krohn of Germany. Each reading has left its mark on the final product.

After all of the above, and above all, it is Barbara Field who once again has not only edited a major publication of mine, but also designed a book for the twenty-first century— a book I believe in.

And finally, let me not forget my husband Arthur Pejsa, who fully supported the journey that spawned the book and the philosophy that underwrote it.

To all of you whom I have named and to those whose names I inadvertently failed to call up, please accept my most sincere gratitude.

Prologue

Once upon a time on the south shore of the great Baltic Sea lay the City of Vineta. Among those who knew that cold, hard sea, the city was said to be world famous. Vineta was also more beautiful than the wider-known City of Constantinople. So said those few who had traveled so far.

In Vineta people from Slavic lands lived side by side with Greeks, Turks, even those barbarous Saxons from nearby lands. The people of Vineta were friendly to outsiders, and they always practiced good manners. Besides, they were successful in business, hallmark of the great Baltic trade centers. Their shops were full of the rarest and most costly goods, brought each year by ships from the far corners of the world.

The inhabitants of Vineta were so rich that the city gates were made of iron plated with brass, while the bells were crafted from silver. In fact, the metal was so available in the city that the most common utensils were made of solid silver. These idols would ultimately destroy this great and beautiful city. Yet the people of Vineta still lusted after more.

Once the citizens had reached the zenith of prosperity, their manners fell by the wayside. They began to quarrel among each other as to who was the richest, hence the greatest. So arrogant had the citizens of Vineta become. In fact they had pushed God's patience too far. On Good Friday those many, many years ago, the city was attacked by a violent storm from the north. Within three days it had sunk to the bottom of the Baltic Sea.

1

Yet we are told, from time to time when the air is damp, the water quiet, and the sun just right, one can look out from the Baltic shore and see the City of Vineta at the bottom of the sea—fine figures in long flowing robes wandering up and down the avenues, sometimes sitting in gold-plated carriages or on great black horses. Sometimes they go cheerfully and busily on their way; sometimes they walk slowly behind a black hearse on its way to a burial. That is when the Vineta silver bells ring out ominously from beneath the sea.

Such is the message from Vineta, its final warning about the wages of arrogance.

Pomorze in Poland

1

Gateway to Poland

It has been more than a decade since the three American visitors previously set foot in Berlin. Yet there he is, Michael Ripke of Heidelberg—their comrade-to-be on this adventure—standing just outside the airport security gate, his automobile little more than a stone's throw away. Little do any of the travelers know that within a few months, Tegel—everyone's favorite airport—will be history. This relic from the time of a divided Germany will be replaced by something larger, grander, safer, and more commercial for the twenty-first century. Perhaps this curious journey through history will be a fitting farewell to that old Tegel of 1975. Curious indeed! It will lead away from the fractured past and, if all goes well, into a brighter future.

Michael does not disappoint. He greets each of the outlanders and leads them to his well-trained Swedish Volvo. Little do any of the visitors yet realize this grand carriage on wheels will become their magic carpet.

THE KISS: Generally the destinations have been mapped out—east to Kleistland and Koszalin in Poland, then south to Dresden, where one can almost touch the future, and finally

5

back to Berlin. At this moment how it might all hang together, how it might point the way to fresh expectations for Europe, is hardly on the minds of the travelers. No time to waste in Berlin now, for they are keeping this city as their dedicated final adventure. As the magic Volvo speeds out of the city—no mean feat in itself—heading northeast and crossing over to Poland south of Szczecin, dark visions of past crossings come to mind. These include long lines of vehicles at the border, questions and inspections by uniformed border guards, and on one early crossing a questionable speeding ticket. With Michael at the wheel, the Volvo crosses without even a slowdown. Entering Poland with a German license plate, the Swedish Volvo just keeps moving, as European autos are wont to do. The first small task is to find a certain flea market near the border. Robert, the inveterate collector among the travelers, stopped there some years earlier. Alas, no flea market. Instead, the Volvo pulls into an outdoor bazaar that features the most inappropriate coffee mugs one can imagine, all at bottom bargain prices. Robert and Jane simply wander about. Helen, however, with Michael as her mug connoisseur and art advisor, begins a search that yields a beautifully shaped specimen on which is printed Gustav Klimt's most famous painting, *The Kiss*.[1] Helen makes her purchase and the *Kiss* mug finds a temporary home in her ample shopping bag.

SZCZECIN: Into the city in the expectation of viewing one of the six memorial plaques placed more than a decade ago across the northwest region of Pomorze. That earlier adventure was a mission of sorts, by twenty travelers of very mixed backgrounds.[2] Three of these sturdy plaques call to memory

---

[1]*Der Kuss* in German. Gustav Klimt was the founder of the Vienna Secessionist Movement and a pioneer in erotica art.

[2]Pejsa, Jane, *Mission to Pomerania, Where Bonhoeffer Met the Holocaust;* see Bibliography.

two synagogues and a Jewish cemetery, all destroyed on *Kristallnacht* ["the night of broken glass"] in 1938. The other three memorialize the ministry and martyrdom of the German theologian Dietrich Bonhoeffer.

The current task lying before the winsome foursome is to locate the plaque commemorating the great synagogue in Stettin. It was mounted on a wall next to the city library, this in a city of more than 400,000 inhabitants. Belatedly, the awareness grows as to how little prepared the group is. Which city library? Which wall? The search for *the* library is turning into a scavenger hunt. Somehow they trust their faithful Volvo, for it magically brought them earlier to the rare Klimt mug. Yet with not a word of Polish among them, even the Volvo seems unable to deliver. Time to find a hotel and an evening meal. In this they are more than successful, with reservations at the Hotel Rycerski—The Knights' Hotel. It is a good choice, with both supper and breakfast served in an attractive dining space on the ground floor—shades of a rathskeller—plus ample protected parking. After this first meal together, the male contingent ventures out, ostensibly to find the library wall and the sought-after synagogue plaque. The search committee does not get very far into the night. Better to check out a local watering hole. It's been a long day.

[Six months after the Volvo adventure, a busload of American tourists from Alabama[3] located the synagogue plaque on the wall next to the Library. They were on a seventeen-day tour that included capitals and other major cities in central and eastern Europe. Szczecin was the last stop before Berlin. One of the tourists, Marie Parsons of Tuscaloosa, Alabama, had with her the book *Mission to Pomerania, Where Bonhoeffer Met the Holocaust*. She was aware that one of the plaques was mounted on a wall

[3]Sponsored by the Osher Lifelong Learning Institute at the University of Alabama.

between the Pomorze library and the site of the destroyed synagogue. She approached the tour guide and inquired as to the possibility of stopping at the Pomorze State Library. The address was not in the book, but with a bit of creativity and his GPS, the guide directed the driver to the spot. Pictures were taken and sent to Jane, proof that the plaque was still alive and well.]

FOLLOWING THE MAP: A bright sunshiny morning, Michael at the wheel and a map on Robert's lap, with the trusty Volvo heading east and south, into the sun. Today, like a magic carpet sailing over an ancient landscape, the Volvo will have to give its all.

From earlier forays into the historic land, the travelers have become acquainted with one Gerhard Rühlow. During World War II, Gerhard was a schoolboy in a small German town called Gross Tychow, one of many such towns in eastern Pomerania *[Hinterpommern]*. The town was hardly a stone's throw from a large German prisoner of war (POW) camp with up to 10,000 prisoners, all English speaking. This camp was Stalag Luft IV, originally a giant clearing in the forest destined to be a German airfield but early on converted to a POW Stalag. In Gerhard's childhood it was forbidden territory, around which youthful imaginations conjured all sorts of sinister purposes. In truth the inhabitants were captured young soldiers—American, British, Canadian, even Australians—who had either fallen out of the sky or been captured on Germany's western front. They were a pitiful lot, homesick, hungry, and most of the time cold in an overcrowded POW enclosure, with a few goons among the guards.

Gerhard has lived in Germany for most of his life—since 1946. That was the year the new Polish Communist government expelled all Germans from their homes, their villages, their towns, and the cities east of the Oder River.[4] By hook or by crook, often on foot, pushing carts containing all their belongings plus young children, whole families were shipped west into Germany under the worst of conditions. From that moment on, Gerhard's old homeland had become part of the *New Territories* in Poland. Nowadays Gerhard's home is in Steinfurt, Germany, as far to the west as is possible without bumping into the Netherlands.

Gerhard is now a retired *Gymnasium* Director. He has developed a lifetime longing for his old homeland. As the years march on, the longing only increases. Over several decades, ever since the Polish government allowed Germans to visit Pomorze, Gerhard has traveled several times each year to Tychowo, once his boyhood home Gross Tychow. It lies almost within shouting distance of Stalag Luft IV. Gerhard is also a frequent volunteer teacher in the Tychowo schools, his subjects ranging from Gross Tychow in earlier times to German-as-a-second-language. A most welcome teacher is Gerhard Rühlow from Germany. In fact, in the summer of 2011, this good man, who for decades has reached out to the people who now dwell in the town of his birth, was granted honorary citizenship. Afterward he wrote:

> This summer the Tychowo city council made me an honorary citizen of their town. Great honor to me, of course. A circle was closed: After World War II the Poles expelled Gerhard Rühlow and millions of his countrymen like cattle. And 65 years later their children and grandchildren call him back and make him one of theirs. More than a symbolic gesture for me, I am back home!
>
> Gerhard Rühlow
> Email dated 11/11/11

[4]Even Stettin, now Szczecin, was incorporated into the new Poland, although this major industrial city lay west of the Oder River.

Stalag Luft IV, POW Memorial

Were it not for a family celebration in Steinfurt, today Gerhard Rühlow would be with the travelers. Instead he has prepared a gift for the Volvo crowd, a hand-drawn map leading from Szczecin to Kleistland by way of Stalag Luft IV. The story of Stalag Luft IV, its POW residents, and the great monument is well told in the author's earlier book, *A Remarkable Journey into the Heart of Europe.*[5] In old Kleistland lie the roots and the heritage of Michael Ripke, captain of the magical Volvo.

[5]Pejsa, Jane, *A Remarkable Journey into the Heart of Europe;* see Bibliography.

2

Heart of Kleistland

The Matriarch's Cottage—once home of the *Matriarch of Conspiracy*[6] and her family. It lies even closer to Tychowo than Stalag Luft IV. As the Volvo makes its way along the county road, the travelers begin to recognize the countryside. They shiver a bit at the turn onto a village road that first passes through the wee town of Krosinko. This was once the Kleist village of Klein Krössin. Behind the village lay an elevated meadow where once stood the "cottage" of Ruth von Kleist, *Matriarch of Conspiracy* and great grandmother of Michael. All that remains now is a green meadow with scattered trees undisturbed by any human-placed ornament. Beginning in 1921 and until 1945, this was the retirement home of Ruth von Kleist. Let the travelers stop for a moment to ruminate on the life—and death—of Ruth's cottage. So is it now known in the literature.

In 1922 a vacant building was especially remodeled for her, with sufficient kitchen and guest rooms to match her

[6]Pejsa, Jane, *Matriarch of Conspiracy, Ruth von Kleist 1867–1945.* In Polish: *W Imie Lepszych Niemiec, Æycie Ruth von Kleist-Retzow 1867-1945.* In German: *Mit dem Mut einer Frau, Ruth von Kleist-Retzow Matriarchin im Widerstand.* See Bibliography.

11

hospitality from the days when she was the widowed matriarch of two great landed estates, Klein Krössin and Kieckow.
At that earlier time she ruled from the Kieckow manor
house. But these were new times in Germany. The tragedies
associated with the Great War, from which few families were
spared, had faded somewhat, in view of the monumental
new challenges before the nation and the people. Ruth's oldest child Konstantin had been killed in the war. Younger son
Hans Jürgen von Kleist, now married, had already taken
over the Kieckow manor house as well as ownership of the
two adjoining estates. That's how things worked in those
days. One generation passed on to the next not only the well-
being of the family, but also that of the land and the villagers
for whom they considered themselves responsible. So began
a new life for Ruth in her cottage in the Kleist village of Klein
Krössin.

Before moving into her new home, Grandmother Ruth
had arranged to have these words carved into the wooden
eave above the cottage entrance—Psalm 31, verse 15:

MEINE ZEIT STEHT IN GOTTES HAND
[My Time Rests in God's Hand]

Over the next quarter century, her hospitality and this
maxim by which she lived would be tested more severely
than she ever might have imagined. The first challenge came
in 1922. European aristocracy was in turmoil after learning
that the deposed Russian Tsar Nicholas Romanov and his
entire family had been executed by the Bolsheviks. Fear ran
rampant that the revolution would spread west into German
lands. However, a mountain of hearsay generated glimpses
of hope, especially in Germany. Most persistent was the
rumor that the Tsar's youngest daughter Anastasia had survived, in other words, that the Russian piece of the House of
Romanov might possibly return to the throne.

Indeed, just two years after the mass execution, in Berlin,
where Russian emigrants swarmed, a young woman

attempted suicide by jumping off a canal bridge. She was res-
cued and taken to a hospital, then to an asylum for the
insane. There she refused to identify herself, thus was given
the name "Fraulein Unbekannt" [Miss Unknown]. Within
the hospital it was gossiped about that Fraulein Unbekannt
was actually Anastasia. Word spread quickly. Suddenly
Berlin society was taking notice of poor Anastasia, daughter
of the late Tsar Nicholas. One Baron von Kleist, an émigré
from "Russian Poland" and a distant cousin of the Kieckow
Kleists, saw his role as benefactor/protector of the young
woman. He contacted Grandmother Ruth's oldest daughter,
Spes Stahlberg, who resided in Berlin. Spes volunteered her
mother's home as a quiet refuge for Anastasia. And so it was
done.

In May of that year, Anastasia was taken directly from the
asylum to Grandmother Ruth's cottage two hundred miles
east of Berlin. Ruth graciously received her, knowing that
with care and friendship Anastasia could recover from whatever ailed her. But it was not to be. The young woman was
condescending to everyone who tried to interact with her,
especially the maid. She had no idea how to behave mod-
estly or otherwise show a bit of respect, attributes demanded
of everyone in the Kleist family circle. One afternoon at tea,
Anastasia suddenly bolted from the tea table. What
prompted this has been lost in history. She retreated to her
guest room and closed the door. When supper was
announced, Anastasia did not respond. When a supper tray
was placed outside her door, she did not answer the knock
nor take in the tray. The following morning, Ruth ordered
the door opened. Anastasia had disappeared, no doubt
through the open window, never to be seen again in
Kleistland. Klein Krössin's hospitality and Ruth's trust had
been violated. Still, in spite of growing evidence to the con-
trary, those of the Kleist clan who had briefly known the
young lady "Anastasia" refused to accept that she was a
fraud.

In those days it seemed all of Pomerania had connections with Grandmother Ruth of Klein Krössin, and more than a few found reason to call at the hospitable cottage. The Anastasia episode simply became an anecdote of some interest.

It was more than a decade since the lost war and the subsequent inflation. A new spirit was in the air. Adolf Hitler and his National Socialist Party were sweeping the nation. Whether in the cities or the rural towns and villages, a fresh wind was blowing. It was difficult for struggling workers and land-poor property owners not to be seduced. Even Grandmother Ruth was not immune. One afternoon right at teatime and unannounced, cousin Ewald von Kleist-Schmenzin[7] arrived on horseback. Ewald was not only a close relative but also a near and dear neighbor, always a welcome guest at the cottage in Klein Krössin. Ruth already had family guests, but a visit from Ewald promised a heightened spirit in any conversation. This time, Ewald was in no mood for chatter. He promptly sat down and opened the book in his hand. Without invitation, he began to read aloud passages from Adolf Hitler's *Mein Kampf.* Using Hitler's own words, Ewald was saying, "Listeners, beware!" Two hours later, having completed his mission, he mounted his horse and returned home, assured that the Kleists of Kieckow and Klein Krössin were of a common mindset with the Kleists of Schmenzin.

In the election of 1933, the Nazi Party won a stunning victory. The first target of the new government was the long-feared Communists. Leaders or not, they were hounded, beaten, arrested, and in some cases taken away, never to return. And the Jews? An increasing level of rage against these people was emanating from Berlin. Too often the attitudes were enthusiastically picked up in Pomerania and else-

---

[7]In 1945 Ewald von Kleist-Schmenzin would be hanged by the Nazis, having been convicted of treason by a kangaroo court.

where. The livelihoods of Jewish families were being destroyed, their small businesses locally boycotted. Civil servants were dismissed from government service, permits to practice medicine or the law terminated, and the children beaten or bullied at school. The life of a Jew in Pomerania had become intolerable. Those with connections abroad and the money to buy their way out were leaving, abandoning their homes and what was left of their businesses. We have a name for what happened to those millions caught in the trap who never made it out—*the Holocaust.*

Yet amidst all this turmoil, a young Protestant pastor, Dietrich Bonhoeffer, was establishing a theological training seminary in a village on the outskirts of Stettin. Finkenwalde was the village name. Ruth had heard of the man and was curious about his independent seminary, which later was forced to go underground. She made it a point to visit him. From time to time, she took several of her grandchildren to the Sunday services at the seminary. Gradually a friendship was growing between this older matron and the young pastor. By and by, she invited her friend to prepare three grandchildren for confirmation, even as she asked him to guide her in her own theological struggles. Always he graciously complied. Over the next few years, Bonhoeffer would spend days and weeks in one of the Klein-Krössin guest rooms, especially after the government declared his seminary illegal. Later it was said Dietrich Bonhoeffer wrote most of his greatest work *Ethics* while staying there. Even after the German invasion of Poland he took time to recoup at Ruth's cottage. By now he was on the periphery of an effort by his brother and brothers-in-law to bring down Adolf Hitler. In 1942, returning from a trip to Sweden on behalf of the conspirators, he swung over to Ruth's cottage, where one of the guest rooms was now known within the family as "Dietrich's room."

By chance Ruth's granddaughter Maria von Wedemeyer was visiting from her home to the south. It had been seven years since Ruth's grandchildren had attended Sunday services at the seminary. Clearly, at seventeen Maria was no longer the rambunctious child of that earlier time. Dietrich asked the grandmother if Maria might accompany him on a walk to Kieckow. He wished to share with Maria's uncle Hans Jürgen the results of his Swedish mission. Of course, permission was granted. A few weeks later he wrote to his good friend Eberhard Bethge:

> . . . I have not written Maria. As things stand, it is impossible now. Even if we never meet again, the delightful thought of those few minutes of high tension will undoubtedly melt once again into the realm of my unfulfilled fantasies, a realm that in any case is already adequately populated.[8]

But Bonhoeffer and Maria did meet again—and again and again. It wasn't long before they became engaged to be married. Maria's mother, Ruth von Wedemeyer, knowing Dietrich was involved in dangerous activities, refused to announce it publicly. In April 1943, Bonhoeffer was arrested. Maria's mother, distraught over her own reluctance in the matter, immediately announced the engagement. The courtship continued through an occasional prison visit and a few letters[9] until the enemy on all sides of the nation had reached Germany's heartland. Exactly two years after Bonhoeffer's arrest, on April 8, 1945, he was transferred to the Flossenbürg Concentration Camp, tried before a "summary" court, and sentenced to death. The following morning, April 9, exactly a month before Germany's surrender, he was executed by hanging.

In February of 1945, just days after the hapless POWs were evacuated from Stalag Luft IV, much against their

---

[8]Pejsa, Jane, *Matriarch of Conspiracy;* see Bibliography.

[9]Bismarck, Ruth Alice von, *Love Letters from Cell 92, The Correspondence Between Dietrich Bonhoeffer and Maria von Wedemeyer, 1943-1945;* see Bibliography.

wishes, the Red Army crashed through into eastern Pomerania and subdued the entire region. Landowners were either arrested or simply shot on the spot. The lands they once ruled were now in possession of the enemy. Ruth's son Hans Jürgen, master of the Kleist estates, was taken to a Moscow prison. Never mind that he had just been released from a Gestapo prison. His wife Marie and Grandmother Ruth were living in the forester's house, totally isolated from others of the family who had fortunately reached the West. The Red Army commandant and his entourage had taken over the Kieckow manor house. Who of the Red Army was living in the cottage at Klein Krössin? That has not been recorded. The following September Ruth was injured in a fall. With no medical care available she soon died.

Exactly when the last remnants of the cottage disappeared is unclear. But that may be the *good* news. In earlier pilgrimages by one or another of the Volvo foursome, Ruth's large and hospitable cottage had gone from its role as a Communist state farm granary to a dark and empty building with many floorboards removed, to a wreck with only a piece of the roof still intact, to a bundle of sticks clearly in need of final demolition, and finally to a lovely, green parklike lawn. Through all the vicissitudes of Ruth's life and all the traumas endured by her cottage, the carved German words, *Meine Zeit steht in Gottes Hand,* remained fixed above the front entrance, just below the eave. Looking up the empty incline, Jane can still imagine the words suspended horizontally in space above what was once the cottage portal. For this Volvo traveler, that is enough.

On the move just beyond the village, the magic Volvo suddenly stops. On the left, in front of a flowering shrub, stands a simple monument with an empty vase before it. Michael is promptly out of the vehicle with his camera. He has been told many times of the terrible accident years ago that killed ten-year-old Ferdinande von Kleist, his mother's cousin from Kieckow. With a bouquet of wild flowers in her hand, she and her father and brother were on the way to Grandmother's cottage in a horse-drawn wagon. Father, with the reins in his hand, sat in the center of the board, one child next to him on each side. When the horse unexpectedly stumbled over a rock, Ferdinande was thrown from the wagon. She died immediately. Of all the loved ones from Kieckow who in the twentieth century were killed long before their time, including three sons fighting for the Fatherland, the death of Ferdinande has been the one longest grieved. On this modest monument are inscribed the words "*Gott rief* [God called] 25. *Mai* 1924." Over many decades, long after Kieckow was transformed into Kikowo, passersby always found freshly watered garden flowers in a glass vase. Today the glass vase is empty. Heinrich von Kleist, the younger of Hans Jürgen's surviving sons, has had a longstanding agreement with a woman from the Krosinko village. But age has caught up with Heinrich. In recent years, it has been ever more difficult to make the strenuous trip from western Germany. And perhaps in the meantime the village woman has died. Yet Ferdinande's memory lives on.

KIECKOW/KIKOWO: Five hundred meters further along the road, the visitors have again stopped, for on the right they recognize the spot that had been missed a decade earlier. Up a gentle incline still stands a grove of ancient oaks with a small stone monument resting in the crotch of the largest tree. Hand chiseled into the stone are the words:

1914 1918 MIT GOTT FÜR KÖNIG UND VATERLAND
[With God for king and fatherland]

A brick walking path leads up from the road to the grove. Mounted at the entrance is a recent plaque, the words in both German and Polish. In this way another bit of memory has been brought into the twenty-first century:

World War I Memorial Oak Grove

In the year 1920 at this place under the protection of an ancient oak grove a symbolic cemetery was laid out—a memorial to the young men of Kieckow and Klein-Krössin who were killed at the front in the First World War.

In the year 1997, thanks to Polish and German cooperation, this symbolic cemetery was restored by the residents of the Tychowo Township as a sign of peace and reconciliation between the Poles and the Germans.

Back on the road toward the historic place once called Kieckow, past large expanses of harvested fields and fresh green growth beyond. The visitors surmise that the harvest, on which all else depends, was good. Presently the buildings stand before them, one or two newer structures, others from Communist times either under repair or simply fading away, and one great brick edifice from Kleist times, still awaiting a final decision by the property owner. But their interest is the manor house, the present and future *Kikowo Pałac*. It seems not to have changed very much in the last few years. Most notable is the absence of obsolete farm machinery, once scattered hither and yon around the landscape, some left over from Communist state farm times. Instead, a new brick entrance drive has appeared lined with flower gardens on both sides, plus larger garden plots beyond. A good omen.

To the visitors' dismay, neither Radek nor Grażyna Romeyko is at home. They are the owners of this grand work in progress. Fortunately one of the Volvo comrades has Radek's cell phone number with her. Michael's cell phone does the rest. Over the phone, Radek promises to return within the hour. In the meantime, an alternative plan has emerged: drive to Tychowo for carry-out sandwiches. It is already long past lunchtime, and in the city of Koszalin the travelers have promises to keep and miles to go. Into the auto and on the way—but not quite!

As they pull out of the drive, another auto, an SUV, also with German license plates, pulls in. The Volvo foursome presumes these are families of villagers from the German times, now tourists visiting the old homeland. Out of curiosity they turn around to the parked SUV just as a group of young adults exits the vehicle. Jane is still sitting on her perch in the back seat of the Volvo, with the door open, when the oldest among the visitors walks directly to her and greets her by name. Then he shows her the book in his hand. It is that little spiral-bound book from 1999, *Mission to Pomerania, Where Bonhoeffer Met the Holocaust.* The inscription inside reads, "To Prof. Peter Zimmermann, Yours, Jane Pejsa."

Now it all comes back to her. They had met a decade ago at an International Bonhoeffer Conference in Berlin. The young men and women in the group appear stunned at this unexpected coincidence somewhere in the backwoods of Poland. Of course they are pleased as well, these students from Leipzig University. They are enrolled in a class on Dietrich Bonhoeffer taught by Professor Zimmermann, the topic: "Practical Christianity." Each semester the climax of the course is a visit to Bonhoeffer sites in Poland. For this, *Mission to Pomerania* is the principal class text. Three of the Volvo bunch as well as Michael's sister Katrina were a part of that early mission to Pomerania. Naturally all four are more than pleased that the little book evolving from it is still fresh in this twenty-first century.

Some minutes later they are back in the Volvo and off to Tychowo for the sandwiches. On return, they find the Leipzig class already on its way to another Bonhoeffer site, while Radek has returned as promised. It is six years since Radek purchased from the government the great house, the farm buildings, and many hectares of the agricultural land. Since then he has leased additional hectares from the government and even purchased a few more. He can now claim he has as much land under cultivation as the Kleists had before 1945. However, where the Kleists had a hundred workers, Radek can afford just four. He is saving to purchase a larger, more automated piece of equipment. Clearly great plans for the *Kikowo Pałac* are not his top priority. Still, since Radek arrived several years ago, the infrastructure has been totally revamped—plumbing and baths in six newly created guest rooms on the second floor, new electric wiring throughout, a central propane gas furnace and baseboard hot water heat, the tin roof repaired, and the distinctive windows that defined the manor house in earlier times now replaced with insulated windows of the exact same design.

Inside, the great front hall with the open corridor above has not changed that much from the visitors' earlier forays. The layers of old linoleum floor coverings have been removed, revealing the original intricately inlaid wood patterns with minimal damage to the surface. Robert marvels at the condition in spite of wartime invasion, occupation, theft, and wanton destruction. A true connoisseur of wood and

Kikowo Pałac, a work in progress

On the right, Robert, Peter Zimmerling, and Jane among a bevy
of students from Leipzig University

inlay, he already visualizes aloud what the great entry hall might once again become—a sparkling inlaid wood floor and a newly crafted solid wood banister ascending the graceful stairway. Imaginations are running wild. The Volvo passengers dare not ask the Volvo master—Michael—for his comments. Perhaps he still holds his mother's childhood memories of the great house, the families that came to call, the weddings, the holiday celebrations, the christenings, even the wakes, for as much as joy was celebrated at Kieckow, family gatherings were too often also about death.[10]

Radek beckons the visitors inside to the grand ballroom next to the old banquet hall, all with glass doors overlooking what was once a glass-covered stone terrace. On earlier visits, visitors were repeatedly told that the collapse of the glass roof over the terrace occurred in 1945 during the Russian occupation. On each subsequent visit, visitors have wondered why the glass shards still lay on the stone terrace floor. Now, in the twenty-first century, joy all around as they observe there are no longer shards of glass on the stone terrace. Through the windows the guests can see a modest tea table on the terrace decorated with a planter of geraniums and flanked by two chairs.

Radek has set a long table in the ballroom with coffee and cookies. He invites his guests to partake. Clearly he has many responsibilities, almost more than he can handle. Grażyna, trained in hotel management, must work also, full time away. She too is supporting the Kikowo enterprise. Radek laments his failure to achieve more than he has already achieved, yet is hopeful his dreams for the *Kikowo Pałac* will eventually come true.

Boarding their gentle vehicle—the occupants take a long look at the church down the village road. The plaque they attached to the stone wall still hangs undisturbed. Can you imagine, that was some fifteen years ago.

[10]Ibid.; *Martiarch of Conspiracy.*

Remembering DIETRICH BONHOEFFER, 1906-1945, a
Christian theologian who stood firmly against Adolf Hitler and
for this was hanged by the Nazis. Bonhoeffer preached a number of times at this church. Here he was supported and protected by the Kieckow landowner von Kleist-Retzow.

— *Travelers from Poland, Germany, and the U.S.A.*

Once again Michael is out the Volvo door with camera in
hand, for behind the old church is a memorial cemetery created by Heinrich von Kleist. First a bit of history: After the
expulsion of the Germans in 1946, the Polish Communist
government embarked on an ambitious plan to remove any
evidence of a past German presence. About all that was left
to do, after renaming towns and streets and whatever, was to
destroy the old German cemeteries. Across the land this
edict was executed one way or another. At Kikowo it meant
digging up tombstones and more. A new Polish cemetery
was created some meters away and the old was just left
there—pieces of individual tombstones visible here and
there, otherwise one big mess. But those times are long
gone. Here and there behind churches, in town cemeteries,
and in country graveyards the Poles are slowly putting things
back together as much as is possible. Enter Heinrich von
Kleist, who has never really emotionally let go of his old
homestead, Kieckow. He hired the Kikowo villagers and
others to find the tombstones, as many as possible, and level
the heap. Not many tombstones could be found intact—in
fact, just four—out of some sixty or more marking the graves
of the once-active cemetery (1885-1945). With these four
Heinrich designed a modest cemetery memorial, topped by
a cross. He has left its care in the hands of the Catholic priest
and the villagers.

Jürgen von Kleist 1854-1897
Konstantin von Kleist 1891–1917
Two people from the old Kieckow village

On his camera Michael now has a photo of the place where his great-grandfather von Kleist and his great-uncle Konstantin von Kleist are buried. No words are spoken here, but perhaps he views this as a closure in the centuries-old history of his forbears, the Kieckow Kleists.

On the way north in the direction of the Baltic Sea: The travelers' thoughts are still with Kikowo—not necessarily with the plucky Kleists nor the martyred Bonhoeffer, but rather with the present owner. The Volvo crowd is still reminiscing on Radek Romeyko's last lament—that he has not yet achieved all that he anticipated. Indeed we wish him success.

The brief Kleistland experience—its history, the old and new monuments, the transformation slowly under way, and Radek's dreams for the future—have added a dimension that would seem inexplicable were it not for Michael and his Volvo. That earlier right turn from the county highway onto the country road was like a journey leading back to past times, then to even earlier times, then forward to modern Tychowo and a Bonhoeffer memorial plaque, interrupted by the empty forester's cottage where the matriarch breathed her last, now without the residue from a Communist state farm. Hither and yon in time, forcing the foursome to imagine a twentieth century of war, peace, and then more war, and then . . . Otherwise the human dramas, the great moments, the destruction, and the slow rebuilding can hardly be described by an ordinary drive in a Swedish Volvo across the Polish countryside. How to explain? Michael's Volvo has been transformed into the travelers' *magic carpet,* through which they not only have been bounced over a country road but also challenged to glimpse an uncommon past through a difficult present, and yet still contemplate a bright future. Sail on!

Koszalin
Tutaj, Here, Hier[11]

---

[11]Here: in Polish, *Tutaj;* in German, *Hier.*

3

Metamorphosis

HOTEL BURSZTYNOWY: Ten kilometers south of Koszalin, way off the main road and surrounded by forest, stands an extraordinary edifice, seemingly a castle out of the eighteenth century. Today it carries the name Hotel Bursztynowy, in English, Hotel Amber or the Amber Palace. Helen and Jane are no strangers to the castle, for back with the earlier mission group of 1999 they spent two nights here. At that time they were told it was built in 1900 by a well-to-do German family von Kamecke. The family had sufficient land and funds to create the opulence of the eighteenth century without sacrificing their modern late-Victorian tastes. And if the castle with its fifty hectares of land were not enough to impress the neighbors, the von Kameckes surrounded their grand residence with expansive gardens, fountains, and even their own little Swan Lake.

Early in 1945, the final invasion from the east subdued the entire region of Pomerania east of the Oder River. No doubt, at least for a moment, some Russian commandant and his entourage must have settled down in the castle, believing themselves ruler of this opulent little empire. What luxury after years of warfare in the field! It is difficult to imagine this moment lasting very long, for early on the Soviet occupation army took over and the great forced exodus of all Germans from these lands commenced. Gradually responsibilities were turned over to the newly formed Polish Communist government. And so, over a period of a year, it was done!

NEW TERRITORIES: If there were vehicles available and money to buy black market gasoline, families might leave by auto. If not, they left by horse and wagon or on foot, many perishing along the way. Very quickly their places and their property were taken over by the new Polish government and assigned to new Polish immigrants—some already living in the neighborhood, having been forced workers on the great German estates, some from the eastern third of Poland, whose lands had been turned over to the Soviets in this great new rearrangement of Russia, Poland, and Germany. Even before the end of the war Poles had come as refugees from parts of Ukraine—survivors of a murderous ethnic cleansing while their German occupiers looked the other way. Others also fled north—landowners great and small. The Soviets found them fair game, for they had strongly resisted land collectivization back to the Russian Revolution. With Germany defeated, the surviving members of the great Polish underground came out of hiding, expecting a hero's welcome. It didn't happen. Wherever the Soviets were in control, these partisan veterans were routinely rounded up and shipped east to one or another of the infamous Siberian Gulags, probably never to return.

And so it was. Even Poland, like Germany, had become a nation of refugees. Either by choice or by command, families made their way north and west into the *New Territories.* No doubt some saw these lands as an opportunity to be seized, while others felt themselves entitled, for they too were refugees from an evil system as well as from war.

Who was to blame for the monumental human trauma unleashed by a simple redrawing of national borders, or to whom should one give credit for providing a new beginning for a long-oppressed people? In war and in peace it always seems to depend on one's point of view.

In Koszalin Communist institutions rapidly evolved, energized by the presence of Communist bureaucrats and enforcers. The Red Army commandant who had ruled from his amber castle had long ago disappeared. The interior was divided into living quarters for refugee families, then later abandoned, and so it remained for years and years. By the time Polish Communism collapsed, the property was in shambles, both within and without. Yet in the mind of a Warsaw investor, the place beckoned. He purchased and restored the great edifice with all its surroundings, adding even more opulence to the mix, and renamed it the *Bursztynowy Pałac*—the Amber Palace.

It is here that the travelers are to meet two gentlemen recommended by a good friend, Rita Scheller, in Germany. Like so many other Germans of a certain age, Rita visits Pomorze from time to time, for this was once her childhood home of Köslin. It is at first unclear as to why this friend insists on such an encounter, but indeed when it comes to Pomorze in Poland, the travelers have learned to follow Rita's advice.

THE ENCOUNTER: The Volvo magic carpet turns from the highway into the forest. It is late afternoon when they find themselves at the front portico of the Amber Palace, just as Helen and Jane remember it from an earlier trip. Two men, each with an umbrella at the ready, await their arrival. Such dears are they, for the visitors are late by almost two hours. The taller one steps forward and calls Jane by name, then administers a great bear hug. Having read *Mission to Pomerania,* he has been forewarned. This is Zdzisław

Bursztynowy Pałac (The Amber Hotel)

Glimpse of the hotel gardens

Pacholski, but the visitors should call him Zibi. He introduces the younger man next to him. This is Father (Ks.)
Henryk Romanik. The priest takes Jane's outstretched hand
and reminds the four that today he is "Henryk."

Zibi interrupts now to bring a message from "Leslie" in
London. The visitors have no clue. Only after Zibi explains
does it all begin to make sense. In recent years Leslie has
been a frequent visitor to Koszalin—"Our famous Jew," says
Zibi, somewhat in jest, although the newcomers will learn
later how true it is. Today Zibi has phoned Leslie in London
and informed him that the unknown "travelers" from the
United States, who placed the plaque in the park near the
synagogue site, are in Koszalin for a visit. Leslie is thrilled—
so says Zibi—and he now sends enthusiastic greetings. For
over a decade he, who was once a child in Köslin, has wondered just who those travelers were.

Zibi cautions the thirsty travelers there is no time for coffee now. He and Henryk have a little tour planned for them
and it is already almost dusk. The travelers obey. In two
automobiles they are off to Koszalin to visit the Old Jewish
Cemetery, the New Jewish Cemetery, and last of all, the synagogue site. Before this moment none of the travelers knew
of either an "old" or a "new" Jewish cemetery, both from
long before the war. They knew of course that such cemeteries would have been victims of the Nazi times, just as the
synagogue was. At the first stop, they find a large area of
green surrounded by an attractive fenced hedge, inside a typical burial marker inscribed "David Baruch." Next to it a
broken stone fragment, more like a square brick—Hebrew
characters and the name "F. Marx." Closer to the enclosure
an inscription in Polish. This was once the Old Jewish
Cemetery. Such a dignified memorial. How did it all come
about? That too shall come to light a bit later. Now a short
drive to a smaller plot of green, on the property of the new
Technical University. Inside a wrought-iron fence is a high-
style cemetery memorial, designed and crafted by the local

sculptor Zygmunt Wujek.[12] Here once lay the heart of the destroyed New Jewish Cemetery.

Finally a short ride back to parking spaces near the synagogue site behind the Park of the Pomeranian Princes, with a shorter walk down into the park. Helen and Jane were here when Mr. Wujek actually nailed the synagogue plaque to the great boulder, a prehistoric relic donated by the city of Koszalin.[13]

> Remembering the Jewish community that dwelled in the Koszalin District until 1942. At this spot stood the largest synagogue. On November 9, 1938, the Nazis burned all the synagogues to the ground and destroyed the Jewish cemetery chapels as well. In 1942, the Nazis expelled the last of the Koszalin Jews, most of them to death camps in the East.
>
> —*Travelers from Poland, Germany, and the U.S.A.*

What fanfare there was at that time—government, newspaper, TV, radio, and the public, with all the expected speeches and even some unexpected. Today, in a much quieter vein, Henryk places a votive lamp at the base of the boulder, then strikes a match. Acknowledging those present and their common purpose of peace and reconciliation, he asks God for a blessing on this place and on this evolving circle of friendship. Quietly they all leave the lighted lamp and return to the vehicles. Henryk's blessing has both sobered the listeners and energized them in their quest to know more.

ZIBI AND HENRYK: A bit later, having registered themselves at the Amber Palace, the visitors join their new friends, now guests, in the seemingly historic cocktail lounge. Historic or

---

[12]Zygmunt Wujek, a well-known regional sculptor, who has created several World War II and Holocaust memorial sculptures, including a huge sculpture at the site of Stalag Luft IV, and who also installed all six memorial plaques from the earlier mission to Pomerania.

[13]Pejsa, Jane, *Mission to Pomerania, Where Bonhoeffer Met the Holocaust, A History and Traveler's Journal;* see Bibliography.

not, it is exactly the right space for the tight little circle. The evening can begin. Wine and juice appear, as well as menus to hold them for the next few hours. Time for a toast to camaraderie and this unexpected encounter. The travelers turn to their guests. "Just who are you, Zibi and Henryk, and who in the world is Leslie?"

Zibi speaks first.

I was born in Koszalin. My parents grew up in south Poland. They were young when the Germans invaded, childhood friends. The Germans shipped my father west to Schleswig-Holstein as a forced worker. He escaped and made his way back to Poland. He did not go home, for he had become a marked man. Rather he joined the Polish Underground—300,000 strong, well-organized and fighting under the auspices of the exiled Polish government in London. What a fierce and dedicated Army! My father, who still lives, has often said, "For six years we fought, we killed, and we died. Yet we won the battle of Poland for the western allies."

Once the Soviets and Polish Underground finally defeated the German Army in Poland, my father and his buddies all came out of the forest, expecting a hero's welcome. Then came the surprise. Those who fought in the Underground were being picked up and shipped east to an uncertain fate. From the Soviet point of view they weren't to be trusted. My father never went back home, even to tell his parents he had survived the war, until after he had fled north to one of the New Territories—*Pomorze.* Eventually he sent for his parents and his childhood sweetheart. They were married, and have lived happily through difficult times as well as good times. My parents feel blessed to live here, God's will. I too am a very fortunate man.

My life's mission now is to bind up the wounds of the past through a wider understanding of our intertwined history and culture. That is the message of my traveling exhibition, *Tutaj, Here, Hier.*

Perhaps you Americans would word it otherwise—"We're all in this together." How does that sound? About the exhibition I shall speak later.

Not waiting for a response, Zibi turns to his friend. "Henryk, it's your turn."

Thank you, Zibi. Like your parents, my grandparents also were refugees from their old homeland. It all began with the Russian Revolution of 1918. My family was from Ukraine with a culture the Bolsheviks—whether Ukraine or Russian—could not abide. Until the collectivization by Stalin and the ruling Soviets, my grandfather's family owned a bit of land. There was great resistance among the landowners, no matter how small their land holding. Thus in 1932, when a drought decimated crops in some areas, Stalin took aim at the entire Ukraine nation. In the disaster areas, the entire crop was requisitioned by force from the farms and people. Some was sent to urban areas and areas where the drought had not struck. Most of it was sold abroad for much-needed foreign currency. Whether 5,000,000 or 11,000,000 Ukrainian people starved to death in this way is still in controversy.

After World War II when the Germans were defeated in Ukraine, my grandparents were pressured to take their family out of Stalin's reach, for who knew how long he would be in power. With many others of their kind, they were delivered in cattle cars to the New Territory of *Pomorze*. I was born a generation later. I made my Abitur in 1978 and was visiting in Rome when Paul II was elected pope. Perhaps the experience propelled me into the priesthood, for this pope represented my own feelings about the Church—as an institution through which men and women can do good work, where openness and dialog are respected, and where everyone has the chance to become a good human being.

Zibi interrupts his friend. "But what about the Jews?" Henryk replies:

Oh, that is a crucial part of all this. I am fascinated with the Hebrew Biblical tradition and the legacy of the Jews in Pomorze, in Poland, and in Europe. In 2006, I published a little book—actually not so little: *O Żydach W Koszalinie [About Jews in Koszalin]*.[14] I read the Psalms daily and I believe strongly in Zibi's mission of peace and reconciliation across Europe.

[14]Romanik, Ks. Henryk, *O Żydach W Koszalinie;* see Bibliography.

4

The Discovery

LOTHAR BARUCH: A pause now while the waiter brings a bit of food. A few quiet minutes of eating until Zibi begins reading here and there from a book he has brought with him. Its title: *Sunday's Child?*[15] The author: a Brit who was once upon a time the child Lothar Baruch, here in Koszalin back when it was Köslin in Germany.

Over the years there had been very little overt anti-Semitism in Köslin. My family had lived there for generations. Before the turn of the nineteenth century they helped organize a Jewish congregation under a renowned Rabbi from the Reform movement. The Synagogue was built in 1886—an impressive house of worship with its beautiful windows and distinctive cupola. The edifice was touted as an architectural wonder in this rather prosaic market town. It even had an organ, unusual for a Synagogue. My father was the organist.

Almost immediately after the national elections of 1933, the pressure on the Jews began. Month by month it escalated. My father noted it first in his business though my parents tried to keep it from us children. As funds withered, my family was forced to move to a smaller residence—a third-floor flat near the

[15]Brent, Leslie Baruch, *Sunday's Child? A Memoir;* see Bibliography.

37

railroad station. As young as I was I too noticed it. One by one my playmates were shunning me. Then they threw snowballs and eventually stones at me. My teacher wore the Nazi uniform to school and bullied me in class. When I came home with a very bloody nose, my parents decided they must act. They pulled me from school and began their search for a safe place. No Jew was really safe without connections abroad or at least in a major city like Berlin.

Very early my father had assured me I was a *Sonntagskind* [Sunday's Child] and would always find good luck. Indeed I was in luck although I didn't realize it at the time. My father knew the director of a Jewish Orphanage in Berlin. I was accepted and in the winter of 1936 my parents delivered me to the orphanage. In 1938 they and my sister followed me to Berlin, in the vain hope there would be safety in numbers, but that was not to be. Their resources had vanished. They lived in a vastly overcrowded *Judenhaus* [Jews' house] while my father labored in a timber factory.

Yet, I must have been a S*onntagskind.* Indeed on December 1, 1938, hardly a month after *Kristallnacht* when all that had defined Jewish history and culture in Germany had been either defaced or destroyed, I was on my way by ship from Amsterdam to London. On this first *Kindertransport* [children's transport] I was one of 200 lucky children to be resettled temporarily in Britain. We were from Germany, Poland, Czechoslovakia and Austria, mostly Jewish, either orphaned or separated from our parents in the chaos following the 1938 Hitler/Chamberlin Munich accord.

I was truly fortunate to be sent to Bunce Court School in Central England. Altogether, thanks to good people in the Netherlands and England, almost 10,000 of us were transported to England in the few months between December 1938 and September 1939, the beginning of World War II.

In the early years of the war, occasional messages came through from my parents in Berlin, no more than 25 words on a form provided by the Red Cross. My parents reported nothing of their own situation, only urged me to work hard and not to forget them, always optimistic and reminding me that I was their Sunday's Child. These messages ceased after the 23rd of October 1942. Only after the war did I learn that my family had been transported to Riga, Latvia. My mother and sister died on October 29, 1942, my father on November 2. Why the discrepancy? Men and women were shipped in separate boxcars. All were shot immediately on exiting the boxcar.

At age 18 I enlisted in the Army, and in January of 1944 reported to military duty as Private First Class *Lothar Baruch.* In 1947 I was mustered out as Captain *Leslie Brent.* The British Army had insisted I adopt a British name. Otherwise, if captured, I could well be shot on the spot. Why did I choose *Leslie?* At that time I was a fan of the British actor Leslie Howard. As to *Brent,* I found the name under the B listings in the London telephone directory and rather liked it.

My University research and my academic career in medical research have been documented elsewhere. Yet, I should like to mention here one event of great importance to me. The 1960 Nobel Prize in Physiology was awarded for a breakthrough in immunology by a team of three English researchers—Peter Medawar, Rupert Billingham, and me—by following the path I devised in my PhD Thesis. Together we cracked the barrier of immunological intolerance in transplant medicine. The Prize, however, was awarded to just one of us— Peter Medawar—while I sat next to him on the podium. Billingham was in the audience. The winner was promptly knighted by the Queen—"Sir Peter Medawar." Sir Peter and I both understood the ways of academia, especially in the upper regions of scientific research.

DR. LESLIE BRENT: So ended the reading from the book *Sunday's Child?* It is already late in the evening and the bartender is closing up. The travelers order a couple of beers, and there is fear they will all fall asleep after this long challenging day. But no, Zibi takes over once more with the tale for which the visitors have been waiting all evening.

It all began simply enough, back in 1988, when we were still under Communism. An acquaintance of mine, Andrzej Michalek, and his wife Malgorzata lived in a third-floor flat not far from the railroad station. It is one of those few buildings that survived the Soviet invasion with almost no damage. One day a fine-looking couple knocked on the door. Malgorzata answered and the gentleman handed her a piece of paper. In Polish it said: "I lived in this flat before the war. Do you mind if we have a look at it for *auld lang syne*?" Malgorzata knew no English. The couple, who appeared to be English, knew no Polish. Nevertheless, with the help of a dictionary, Malgorzata was able to convey an invitation for the following afternoon when her husband also would be present.

And so it happened. The following day Leslie and Joanne Brent of Birmingham, England, came to Leslie's former home for coffee and a freshly baked cake. It was a moment of *déjà vu* for Leslie, seeing once again the blue floor tiles, each with a shell in the middle, not even cracked, and the great tile stove that heated the flat in winter. He stifled his emotions as he asked if he might sit for a moment on the balcony chair. He would like to see the view north toward the lake and the great Baltic Sea beyond. Granted. Leslie tried to explain to the host and hostess his immense gratitude for this privilege. As a child he had spent hours on this balcony, dreaming of being a sailor one day. Oh how he longed to travel the seas and discover new places.

As the Brents were leaving, Leslie gave the Michaleks his card, with all the information they would need if they ever visited England. On the rear side in pencil he wrote "Lothar Baruch." Back on the street Leslie said to his wife, "I shall never again come back here. It is almost too painful for me." But as it turned out, Leslie Brent's "final" visit was only the beginning.

In 1998, I helped curate an exhibition on "Anne Frank's Story for Today." It was initially designed for high school students in Koszalin, most of whom had never heard of Anne Frank. After the exhibition in Koszalin, we sent it to other cities in Poland. Altogether at least 30,000 people viewed it. As you may know, in Poland it had not been common to speak about the Jews, even among neighbors, for one never knew what the reaction would be. Many people harbored negative thoughts. However, after the Anne Frank exhibition there was a sea change in attitudes.

About that time a friend of mine found a tombstone submerged in a stream near the site of the Old Jewish Cemetery. On it were some Hebrew characters and the name *David*

Baruch, all chiseled into the surface. My friend took the stone monument to our Heritage Museum. Then fortunately he phoned me and I contacted the newspaper, which published an article with a picture of the tombstone.

And now the discovery. The Michaleks had recently built a new home in the neighborhood where my wife and I also have a home. Malgorzata read the article about the *David Baruch* tombstone. Now she dared tell me what had happened ten years earlier when a professor from England visited her and had written the name *Lothar Baruch* on the back of his card. She gave the card to me and told me the entire story of Professor Leslie Brent's visit. I promptly phoned the professor at his office in Birmingham and told him about the discovery of the *Baruch* tombstone. After he recovered from the shock, he was able to discern that David Baruch was his great uncle, the brother of his grandfather. His own grandfather was buried in the New Jewish Cemetery.

This discovery prompted a citywide effort to restore the Old Jewish Cemetery as a memorial. Since then Professor Brent has visited Koszalin several times. Of course he came for the dedication of the Old Jewish Cemetery, then later to receive an award from the City of Koszalin, and finally to show his son and second wife Carol something of his long-lost roots.

Since the discovery, each year on November 9 we have a memory walk. It begins at the plaque in the Park of the Pomeranian Princes near the synagogue site, placed there in 1999 by you and the other unnamed travelers. After a blessing, we walk to the rededicated New Jewish Cemetery on the hill, finally to the Old Jewish Cemetery, then back to the synagogue plaque for a final benediction.

And one last thing: Koszalin's famous Jew now carries an additional name. He is Leslie *Baruch* Brent, which means he belongs to us.

THE EXHIBITION: Zibi now expands on his life's mission:

Fortunately here in Koszalin we become more and more aware of the German community that once dwelled here. In fact, the traveling exhibition I have created with photos from then and now is inspired by my belief that both Poles and Germans are

Ks. Henryk Romanik with the foursome viewing the resurrected "F. Marx" and "David Baruch" burial stones at the Old Jewish Cemetery

Zdzisław Pacholski (Zibi) with Henryk at the plaque commemorating the destruction of the Koszalin synagogue, *Kristallnacht* 1938

ready to build a community of understanding. We peoples, through our culture and our history, are intertwined and have been for centuries.

As a professional photographer-researcher, I have accumulated several thousand photos relating to Pomorze and beyond—both from German times and today. I was looking for a method to incorporate the voices of a diverse group of refugees—beginning with those who during Stalin times survived ethnic cleansing of Poles in the Ukraine, then moving on to more of the same during war, plus the overwhelming massacre by Nazi Germany of the Jews and others in the *Holocaust,* then followed immediately after the war with the expulsion of all Germans from Poland's New Territories by the Communist government.

I selected five people, either survivors of the times or the children of survivors—each person representing a class of refugees as I have described these. I asked each one to select several photos and write down what each photo suggested to him or to her. I had no idea what to expect though I believed in what I was doing. Some photos showed lovely scenes, long before and shortly after 1946. Others were unsettling, for instance, an older man and woman standing before their home with all their earthly possessions packed in two small suitcases. Presumably they were awaiting transportation for their expulsion. Other pictures suggested a more optimistic view of past, present, and future. Some were much more recent photos, even good times. Yet universally among the photo essays was the notion of leaving the broken past, acknowledging evil done and letting its disintegration fade away while the present becomes ever stronger and more vivid. Two of the selected photos suggested horrific events—*The Ramp*[16] at Auschwitz

---

[16]*The Ramp* was located just outside the gate at Birkenau (Auschwitz II). Carloads of Jews, gypsies, homosexuals, war prisoners, and other "undesirables" exited the cattle cars onto a ramp. An SS officer, probably a doctor, pointed left or right for each prisoner. To the left was the huge gas chamber, camouflaged as a shower area and designed to process 6,000 people in a day. Virtually all women and children were sent to the left. To the right were sent the most able-bodied men for hard labor, starvation, and in all cases eventual death.

and the broken city of Kalisz.[17] Even here the essayists suggest a rebirth while acknowledging the evil as it disintegrates into the past.

Recently I was in Kalisz visiting a friend. We walked the streets of a town still not reborn. Yet the signs were there—repairs to the ancient castle that once dominated the cityscape, renewal of a few buildings, and street improvements. All that is missing is the population. Kalisz still suggests death. The young people leave for opportunities in Germany and other parts of Poland. Perhaps one day they will return.

Out of the photos and the essays, thanks to all five of the participants, we have created an exhibition. We are taking it to others on both sides of the Oder and Neisse rivers. We intend to instill a sense of our common culture, our history, and our future together in Europe. In other words, to further build community through an exhibition of words and pictures. *Tutaj, Here, Hier!* All of the text is in three languages—Polish, English, and German. It has already had showings well beyond Koszalin—in Warsaw, in the Netherlands, in Berlin, and in other cities across Germany—always with great receptions, generally with television interviews. One day soon it will travel to London.

I see an expanding *Tutaj, Here, Hier* now as my life purpose.

From a radio interview in Koszalin at the opening of the Exhibition. Consul General Joachim Bleicker, representing Germany in Gdañsk, Poland, is speaking.

---

[17]Kalisz, Poland. Very close to the German border in 1939, a town of some 43,000, more than half of them Jews. Captured by the Germans in the first days of World War II, the massacre of Jews promptly commenced—murder and deportation of 30,000 Jews. By the end of the year, the town was declared *judenfrei* [free of Jews]. Non-Jewish Poles had conspired with the German occupiers, but once the Jews were gone they too were deported east to unknown fates. The town was promptly declared part of Germany, a new homeland for German immigrants. After the war, the town and much more reverted back to Poland. A few Jewish survivors returned, but soon left again.

Evening in the bar of the Amber Hotel

The title of the exhibition is clear and simple: *"Tutaj, Here, Hier."*

It defines the place—the region—in which we find ourselves. In three languages the title hints that the theme is not one-dimensional, but rather has many aspects.

These are the languages of the participants in the project—they who speak Polish, English, and German. Indeed, in combination they help us understand the temporal dimension.

In this region German as the language of the past, Polish as the language of the present and English as the link and a vision of our common future within worldwide globalization. *Or* as a warning—and with good reason—of continuing old patterns. Generations of traditions that grew over centuries have been broken. They are now being newly laid or adapted [to a new environment].

This Exhibition is in response to this complicated mix, which for me includes as much a piece of loss as it does a new Fatherland. I am convinced that the beauty of the exhibition lies in its photos and stimulating text. It will become the impulse for many people to see clearly who they are, whence they have come, where they find themselves this day and where they are going.[18]

TO THE FUTURE: Time to say good night to the travelers' newest best friends, Henryk and Zibi, and of course to send greetings to Leslie in Birmingham, England. It becomes a bit emotional, although the visitors promise they all shall meet once more in this world. Time also for the four travelers to retire. Tomorrow after breakfast they are off on their next adventure, rather their continuing adventure—west and south to the land of the Saxon princes.

After a long and pleasant drive from Koszalin, over the Oder River but avoiding Berlin, the Volvo brings them happily to their next destination—the *Hotel am Bonhoefferplatz* in historic Dresden. Along the way a stop for lunch at the restaurant *Zur Reuse*[19] ["to the fish trap"] in the heart of the Spreewald, clearly a vacationland of forests, fields, and water. Like many other tourist places in the region, the distinctive feature of this eatery is the pleasant canal flowing leisurely beside the outdoor tables. The ambiance suggests fresh fish, but no, the foursome becomes tantalized with the menu offering of "regional food," which includes "soft sausage." Somehow they all fall for the soft sausage. Next time no doubt they will stay with the fish.

[18]Translated from the German by Jane Pejsa.

[19]See page 136.

Dresden in Saxony

5

A Word About Saxony

One might ask the question: What is so special about Saxony and the Saxons? From time to time one hears comments such as, "Those Saxons made the best Nazis and later—much later—when it seemed opportune, they made the best Communists."

An old friend, Martin Hüneke of Bad Iburg, Germany, is cosmopolitan to the core. He is a theologian and a scholar, especially when it comes to the life and times of Dietrich Bonhoeffer. As such, he has accompanied some of the mission travelers on earlier trips to Pomorze. Yet Martin confesses to being an "old Saxon" by birth and takes issue with prejudices among his north German neighbors. He asserts that Saxons often sense what seems to be the next opportunity, then with a burst of enthusiasm readily sign on. For instance, after World War I, in the worst of economic times, whole corps of citizens enamored with the promise of Marxism marched daily in the streets across Germany. Dresden and Leipzig in Saxony became hotbeds of enthusiastic Marxists. By 1933, however, when the Nazis took power, loyalties quickly changed. The Nazis had framed themselves as a national "workers party." It was not difficult to incorporate a ready-made corps of Marxist Saxons. The reasons may well have included the promise of economic opportunity under the Nazis. For these erstwhile Marxists to do otherwise suggested the likelihood of arrest, a short time of mistreatment in prison, then internment in a concentration camp. After the Nazis took power, from the first moment on, those identified as Communists had the most to fear.

6

The Nazi Times

AND THE JEWS: Beginning in 1933, it was a slow but steadily increasing squeeze, energized by negative and highly inflammatory anti-Semitic propaganda. The new government badly needed money and perceived an easy source to be the Jews, especially those with assets. A Jew who succeeded in obtaining an entry visa from another country was permitted to leave Germany, but only after paying a hefty sum to the government—a sort of exit tax. A Jew's exit tax depended on assets. Bank accounts of Jews were blocked and permission was needed to release any funds to the owner of the account. Once-wealthy Jews were left with little more than funds to buy steamship tickets. Still many did leave, in spite of severe immigration restrictions, especially those of the United States.

THE SQUEEZE: As the months went on, Jews in the government civil service were fired, their careers destroyed, licenses to practice the law or medicine denied, and university professors gradually laid off, for reasons both obvious and opaque. Such was the case of one Dr. Victor Klemperer, chair of Romance languages and literature as well as professor of philology and philosophy at the Technical University

Dresden Postcard 1935: Semper Opera House, Bellevue Hotel,
Elbe River

in Dresden. In 1935, at age fifty-four, he was given a choice:
either resign now at a reduced pension or stay on and receive
an even more reduced pension. Professor Klemperer chose
to resign.

He and his wife Eva had built a modest home in the
nearby village of Dölzschen—the address, Am Kirschberg 19.
It was a lifelong dream house. Professor Klemperer was rec-
ognized across Europe as the prime researcher, lecturer, and
publisher of books and other papers on the French
Enlightenment, especially Voltaire, of whom the professor
was a devotee. Yet he saw himself as unquestionably a
German intellectual. His whole professional career had been
based on what he considered his German character and his
German heart. He proudly wore the Iron Cross from World
War I. Years earlier he had converted to Protestant
Christianity.

Klemperer suffered greatly under this utter debasement of his true identity. He vowed to continue his research and to write, mainly on two manuscripts in his field that begged to be completed. Besides, he would continue to keep the diary he had begun in January of 1933. Of course he didn't expect to publish the diary; in fact, he kept it hidden. For sure the nonsense created by the Nazis would be short-lived. The government couldn't hang on for more than a year, three at the maximum. In many ways Professor Klemperer was clairvoyant. He could almost predict the next proscription against the Jews, experiencing the terror even before it arrived. In his diary he wrote, "that was the worst."

A MIXED MARRIAGE: As the months went by, a Nazi doctrine of marriage evolved. There were two kinds of persons— *Jewish* and *Aryan.* This must be fully stated on personal identification cards. These IDs were to be carried at all times. At first it was not clear which was which. Over the last hundred years, Dresden had become a city of mixed religions and mixed marriages, typical of large cities—half-Jews, quarter-Jews, and lower-fraction Jews abounded.

Now the regulations were specific. A person with at least one "voll-Jew" grandparent was a Jew. His or her identification card was marked with a single letter "J." In the words of the Third Reich, Victor's wife Eva Klemperer was an Aryan and Victor a Jew. Through his marriage he was, however, officially classified as a "privileged" Jew. This fact would save the lives of both Eva and Victor when it came to the final cataclysm.

KRISTALLNACHT: By the end of 1938, whatever pressure had earlier motivated Jews to leave their homeland was dwarfed by what happened on the night of November 9/10 of that year. This was *Kristallnacht,* or "the night of broken glass," and it changed everything for those Jews still left in Germany.

On that fateful night more than 1,000 synagogues in Germany were burned to the ground, 7,000 Jewish businesses destroyed, hundreds of Jews beaten on the street or in their homes, others snatched up and sent to concentration camps.

In short order, Jews were forbidden to drive or even own automobiles, use public libraries, attend the cinema, use public swimming pools, enter parks, own telephones, radios, or typewriters, even to own pets, buy tobacco, cigarettes, or flowers. Their food rations were reduced beyond the reductions for Aryans. Increasingly prohibitions continued even as one by one the Jews conveniently disappeared—arrest for reason or no reason, prison, concentration camp, and in the early days their remains returned to the surviving family in a small urn.

7

The Klemperer Diaries

All of this degradation was experienced by the Klemperers and duly recorded in Victor's diary—in the early years it was self-typed, but after confiscation of his typewriter, handwritten. Following are selections from the published Klemperer diaries.[20] Shortly after the German invasion that initiated World War II, the government declared that Jews must move into designated apartment houses for the duration, to be under better control. Between 1940 and 1945, the Klemperers would be resettled in a series of three such houses, each more crowded than the former—the crowding only relieved from time to time when groups of up to fifty residents were summoned for deportation.

> OUR JEWS' HOUSE [*JUDENHAUS*]—*New Year's Eve 1939:* This Christmas and New Year's Eve are decidedly worse off than last year. We are threatened with the confiscation of the house—despite that I feel better than I did then; there is movement now, and then everything was stagnating. I am now convinced National Socialism [Naziism] will collapse in the coming year.

[20]Klemperer, Victor, *I Will Bear Witness 1933-1941,* translation © 1998 Martin Chalmers, Random House of Canada Ltd., Toronto; also Klemperer, Victor, *I Will Bear Witness 1942-1945,* translation © 1999 Martin Chalmers; ibid.

Perhaps we shall perish with it, but it will certainly end, and with it one way or another, the terror. Shall we manage to save [our] house and cat, however?—We have lit our nice Christmas tree every night and intend to do so again today. I believe the pograms of November '38 made less impression on the nation than eliminating the bar of Christmas chocolate.

April 19, 1940: Dölzschen town forced an agreement on me through the district Nazi headquarters. According to it, our house is to be rented out for two years. I am not allowed to enter it without permission from the local authority, I am not allowed to make any demand on the tenant without the government's permission. The contract is such a piece of extortion and instrument of future harassment that we wanted to sell the house right away. But we would lose everything. Estreicher advised me [to sign], so we did. Estreicher is a Jew, but he is in charge of allocating accommodations. His advice not to sell the house certainly contradicts his Nazi instructions. They want Jewish private houses sold "voluntarily," in order to avoid the odium of expropriation. Perhaps I shall also be deceived by Estreicher, but what difference does it make? I am under any circumstances helpless and without rights.

May 11: Yesterday the offensive through Holland and Belgium began "at dawn." Naturally a "counterattack" to "ward off the hostile invasion at the last moment." The whole staging, Hitler's proclamation with the famous "thousand years," his assumption of command of the operation (!) shows that everything will be decided now. If he does not win, he will fall. In terms of the philosophy of history Montesquieu is right: "The Republic would have fallen, even if Caesar had not crossed the Rubicon." True—but when would it have fallen? Historical development takes more time than an individual human being has. I fear Hitler's halo of invincibility.

May 26: 15B Caspar Friedrich Strasse. A handsome villa, too cramped, too "modern" in style, stuffed full of people, who all share the same fate. All of it amid an abundance of lilac, chestnut blossom, spring in all its forms. Really splendid the magnificent gardens on wide Waterloo Strasse. In short Dresden at its best. So far so good; otherwise a most terrible state of affairs; there are many moments in the day when one would wish to be dead and buried. The Third Reich's prospects of victory are very high, to say the least.

July 6: New prohibition for Jews: Not allowed to enter the Brühl Garden or other parks. I test my own heart. I always declare: "One day the J will be my alibi." But it is always horrible for me to show the J card. There are shops that refuse to accept the cards. There are always people standing beside me who see the J. If possible I use Eva's "Aryan" card in shops that are unfamiliar to me. Apart from that Eva is now on a wearisome hunt for clothing [ration] point cards, in order to get something by way of exchange for me for my raggedness.

July 9: My idea of Germany was lost years ago, and now France! As if it were Czechoslovakia or a small state in the Balkans. Two million surrender, Metz is captured by a handful, Belfort does not defend itself at all. And now they are convening a general assembly in order to make their constitution "totalitarian," threaten death for anyone who as a Frenchman goes on fighting in the English army, turn themselves into a German protectorate. What is left of my idea of France?

NEW PROHIBITIONS—*August 11, 1940:* All Jews have been given notice that they are forbidden to have a telephone. We are ever more closely confined. A ghetto has been set up in the General Government area of Poland and the Jews have been ordered to wear Zion armbands; they are doing forced labor. [In Germany] Children of mixed race are no longer being admitted to secondary schools. Officially it was still allowed; but a director who permitted a mixed-race child among his pupils would earn a complaint to the Party from Hitler Youth and parents. Thus one rector has been dismissed for being "pro-Jewish," as a result of which no headmaster accepts a mixed-race child anymore.—Everything points to a constant worsening situation for Jews.

August 30: Hitler's most recent piece of harassment, the limitation of shopping hours; I am allowed to go shopping only between three and four (Saturday eleven and twelve). I am more irretrievably isolated than all other members of the Jewish Comumnity. Every day there are rumors about new torments, and so far most have come to pass. The latest said: Yellow armbands to distinguish the Jews, further the confiscation of Jewish sewing machines and typewriters.

October 25: Yesterday evening eighty mass rallies: "Everything for victory." Slogan of the Home Front. Air raid warning at three A.M. The fourth in Dresden, again without anything further happening and only of short duration. Six hundred thousand people have had no sleep. And each one of those six hundred thousand knows the aircraft flying past overhead have gotten down to business somewhere else.

December 20: New intensification of Jewish harassment: After eight o'clock confined in the apartment itself. Visiting other residents of the house, spending time in the entrance hall or on the stairs is prohibited.

January 21, 1941: The naïveté of the American literature. Naïveté in the best sense, even where it is kitsch. Even Hollywood is naïve. They are a new nation, and they are *one nation, one* although mixed from a hundred races, tribes, cultures; they utterly contradict the racial theory of the Nazis. I would so much like to go deeper into American literature. If I could only speak English. Impossible wish: to crisscross the USA for a whole year in my own car. To speak English during this time, only read newspapers, magazines, go to talkies. Then study and write about American literature in my own house on the American East Coast. I am going to be sixty and my heart rebels every day.

February 20: Since Friday morning upset and completely taken up with a letter from Dölzschen authorities, the car must be sold within a week. I surrendered my driving license in '38. Compulsory sale had been in force for one year, they were under no obligation to show me the order. I handed in my registration card and took it to the local Opel man. Result: Because taxes are owed on it, the car would not find a buyer who would pay more than a junkyard. He has a friend who is a secondhand dealer, trustworthy and decent-thinking, who will not exploit my predicament and the fact that I am no Aryan. Agreement by phone: Meincke, the dealer, will take possession of our jalopy, as junk. How much extreme bitterness is contained in this entry, what robbery and what an irreparable loss. When will I ever have a car again?

June 22 [Invasion of Russia]: Russia! Kreidl came by in the morning. "It's starting with Russia." Went to the restaurant in the railroad station to listen to Goebbels' speech. General cheerfulness of the populace: "Triumphant we shall conquer France, Russia and the whole wide world." A new entertainment, a prospect of new sensations, the Russian war is a source of new pride for people, their grumbling of yesterday is forgotten . . .

August 22: Lightning war [Blitzkrieg], final battle—superlative words. War and battle are no longer enough. At the same time the megalomania of numbers: "The enemy's unimaginable bloody losses." Also 1,250,000 prisoners, etc. "Unimaginable" in German military bulletin! Not a word about our own losses.— But *vox populi:* "Russia will be finished in two weeks." Perhaps *vox populi* really is right. Frau Voss always making acquaintances, meets a young girl, a student, working in the Propaganda Ministry at the moment. She says: "Russia is terribly difficult, after all. In recent days it has been causing us a great deal of concern."

THE JEWISH STAR—*September 8, 1941:* The Official Gazette of the Reich announced the introduction of the yellow Jewish armband. That means upheaval and catastrophe for us.

September 15: The Jewish armband comes into force on the 19th. At the same time a prohibition on leaving the environs of the city. I myself feel shattered, cannot compose myself. Eva now firmly on her feet, wants to take over all the errands from me. The newspaper justification [for the yellow star]: After the army had learned, through Bolshevism, the cruelty, etc., of the Jew, all possibility of camouflage must be removed from the Jews here, to spare the comrades of the people [non-Jews] all contact with them.—The true reason: fear of Jewish criticism because things look bad in the East or at least are at a standstill.

September 18: Today the Jews' star. Frau Voss has already sewn it on, intends to turn her coat collar back over it so that it won't be noticed. Allowed? I reproach myself with cowardice. Why? Because I am ashamed. Of what am I ashamed?

October 4: Favorable experiences with a star. A child of former acquaintances had run away full of fear: "Ugh, a Jew!" Horrified, the mother apologized, he had not heard it at home—presumably at kindergarten—the child's fear could not be pacified. Another experience, this while shopping: An elderly woman, selling from a handcart. "Can I have some of the large radishes?"—"But of course!"—I glance longingly at the tomatoes, forbidden "goods in short supply." "They're not to be had without a card, are they?"—"I'll give you some, I know how things stand." She makes up a pound. Then reaches under her cart, pulls out a handful of onions, which are very rare: "Hold out your bag—so that's 60 pfennigs altogether."

November 1: Was for the first time subjected to some abuse the day before yesterday. At Chemnitzer Platz a group of Hitler Youth cubs. "A yid, a yid!" Yelling they run toward the dairy I am just entering, I can still hear them shout and laughing outside. When I come out, they are lined up. I look calmly at their commander, not a word is spoken. A couple of hours later, at Lange's nursery, where I am fetching sand for Muschel [the cat]. An older worker. "You, mate, do you know Herrschmann?—No?—He's a Jew too, porter like me. I just wanted to say: It doesn't matter about the star, we're all human beings, and I know such good Jews." But which is the true *vox populi?*

INVENTORY—*November 9, 1941:* We are often downstairs with the Kreidls, or they come to us. Paul Kreidl, doing heavy laboring constructing railway lines, the Jew's star on his sackcloth smock. The deportations to Poland continue.

November 30: Emigrants—Reich law since two days ago—declared stateless, their blocked accounts seized. I have the impression that terror and chaos are getting worse day by day. Ever new battles in the East, even though Russia is supposed to have been annihilated long ago.

December 4: The diary must be out of the house. Yesterday Paul Kreidl brought news that a circular was on its way: Inventory of household effects. That means confiscations, perhaps also deportation. A house search can be expected immediately after the inventory statement. Eva is therefore to take my diaries and manuscripts to Annemarie [former housekeeper]. If necessary I shall have to stop diary notes altogether. Today I shall leave my personal documents to be photocopied, since all documents are likely to be confiscated.

December 9: Big news yesterday evening. Japan declared war on the USA on the 8th or 7th. Now all opinion in the USA will be for war with Germany. The military bulletin says henceforth it is necessary to reckon on the winter and otherwise rest. Therefore the attack on Moscow and Petersburg appears to have been unsuccessful. And how often have they already said Russia completely beaten. Exactly like last year—"England is already dead."

December 23: In yesterday's newspaper, a call by the Führer and Goebbels to give all fur and woolen things, which could be spared, for the Eastern Front; to the Jews, however, insofar as they wear the star, all fur and woolen things to be handed over "without compensation" by 5:00 this afternoon—"the authorities will carry out checks later."

December 31: It was our most dreadful year, dreadful because of our own real experience, more dreadful because of the constant state of threat, most dreadful of all because of what we saw others suffering (deportations, murder) but at the end it brought optimism—I quoted widely—*nil inultum remanebit*—head held high for the difficult last five minutes!

On the twentieth of January 1942, the government officials responsible for policies relating to the Jews met in a villa at Wannsee, a suburb of Berlin. The plan, later approved by Hitler, was announced under the words: "The final solution to the Jewish question." According to the surviving Wannsee Protocol, those Jews still left in Europe would be deported to German-occupied areas in eastern Europe. They would be used for road-building projects, and would presumably die during their time of labor, the remnant to be done away with on completion of the projects. However, the German lines in the east were being gradually pushed back by the Soviets, no time for road-building projects.

8

The Final Solution

DEPORTATION—*January 13, 1942:* Paul Kreidl tells us—a rumor, but it is very credible and comes from various sources—evacuated Jews were shot in Riga [Latvia], in groups, as they left the train.

January 17: Evacuation of all the Jews here on the coming Wednesday, exception anyone who is over sixty-five; who holds the Iron Cross, First Class; or is in a mixed marriage, including one without children. Point 3 protects me—for how long? Terrible scenes of despair are said to be taking place in the factory where very many Jews work. Married couples, but parents and children are separated without pity. Thus the fifteen-year-old daughter of a pharmacist remains behind here alone. The evacuation order appears to have originated from a Reich department and to have landed on Saxony without warning.

January 19: The Gestapo has struck twenty from the list of those to be reclaimed by Zeiss-Ikon [factory]. In total, 250 people will after all leave here on Wednesday. Among them Paul Kreidl, a very heavy blow to his mother. Among them is also said to be a mother with three small children, the youngest a baby two months old.

January 20: Yesterday with the Kreidls downstairs until midnight. Eva helped sew straps for Paul Kreidl, so that he can carry his suitcase on his back. Then a feather bed was stuffed, which one has to hand over (and apparently one does not always see again). Today Paul Kreidl carted it out on a little handcart.

January 21: Before a deportee goes, the Gestapo seals up everything he leaves behind. Everything is forfeit. This morning a kind of visit of condolence to Paul's mother.—The transport now includes 240 persons; there are said to be people among them who are so old, weak, and sick that it is unlikely that everyone will still be alive on arrival. (Continuing severe cold.)

January 31: Since yesterday a new, extremely depressing difficulty: [Our] house in Dölzschen appears to be or is finally lost. Notice of calling in the mortgage on July 1. My plot of land is completely neglected, repairing the damage is likely to cost 2000M. A trustee will have to be appointed, who is to effect the "Aryanization" of the house. So not only will the house be taken away from me, a further 2000 Marks for future repairs will be deduced from the fixed minimum price. We shall be beggars. What hits me hardest about this business is Eva's bitterness.

February 15: Yesterday, February 14, the first day clearing snow from eight till two, but this coming week it will probably last from eight or half past eight until five o'clock, plus a march of one hour there and one hour back. Yesterday left after seven o'clock in the gray of dawn, almost darkness, with Dr. Friedheim. Snow-covered streets unrecognizable. Dr. Friedheim fell twice, once very heavily. A pitiful group assembled—one rupture, without rupture belt, one cripple, one hunchback, seventeen "older" men should have come, two had not turned up, three were sent away, of the remaining twelve several over seventy, I at sixty literally the youngest.

February 19: Yesterday and today marched off to Langemarckstrasse, continued along the main road in the direction of Kaitz. Different foreman, different supervisor, again both were very humane and anti-Nazi. "Don't say we treated you well, rather say we were bad; otherwise we'll be in trouble. Look, I can't tell you to work more slowly, you have to know that yourself." The foreman always with us. Fifty-five, glassblower until 1930, then unemployed for a year, since then municipal worker. Social Democrat, trade unionist, house searched in '33. Entirely for us. Yesterday a young woman or lady stopping: "But that's too hard for you (meaning all of us)."—"You're too old, and one can see you have other professions (with passionate emphasis)." "*That's* what Germany has come to!"

March 1: In the morning the milkmaid refused to come up. She is no longer allowed to deliver to Jews' houses.

July 1: Yesterday morning I was going to the letter box, Frau Ida Kreidl told me: "Now I have lost everything. My children in Prague are also being evacuated." She has a married daughter there, her grandson is ten years old. The family is being sent to Theresienstadt, from there into the unknown. Her son Paul has been gone since January. In the evening Elsa Kreidl appeared: Her husband's urn and nine other' urns have arrived for interment. Friedheim and Ernst Kreidl will be interred at half past nine on Sunday. Now, that is grotesquely awful. Eva and I had the same thought. Just as the two of them liked to sit together on the garden bench, so now their urns stand side by side. Kreidl's path to death began six months earlier. Friedheim caught up with him. The Jewish layer-out said that Friedheim had hanged himself. (It was said that a rope is placed in the prisoners' cells.)

August 24: In the evening we were once again caught up in the evacuation. But Ida Kreidl was very calm. Subsequently I saw her weeping after all. Across the keyhole on the ground-floor flat with four red Gestapo paper seals. Everything now belongs to the state, the owner is absolutely stripped naked. Frau Kreidl is wearing five dresses one on top of the other, likewise, she says, six drawers and six pairs of socks. And then she still owns what could be fitted into a suitcase and a handbag. She was still brave when she took her leave of us—I was again embraced and kissed. The fifty people have to be at the Community House at two. They spend the night on deck chairs, evacuation early in the morning—next group two weeks after. The sealed ground floor, the solitude in the house—the ending of our evening visits downstairs.

August 25: This morning a young, blond, very pleasant-looking lady appeared. She wanted to visit Ida Kreidl, had heard and was appalled by the seals. Frau Dr. Strüver—she had sometimes exchanged a few words with Ida Kreidl. I brought Frau Strüver up to our apartment, we told her about the conditions and events of recent months. She offered us help if there was anything she could usefully do (she had wanted to help Frau Kreidl out with a suitcase); she then asked me to forgive her if she did not greet me on the street. I told her—and they were not just words—it always made me happy when I met with Germans who made it possible for me to preserve my feeling for Germany. . . .

THE REMNANT—*February 5-12, 1945:* Eva came to fetch me upstairs. She was admired for her courage.—Why courage?—It was said that Aryan wives were forbidden to visit Jews, even those in mixed marriages. We had not heard anything about it. On the other hand we had been warned—secret order—Jews not to talk in groups, not even in twos, on the street, above all to display a cheerful and even "triumphant expression." More threatening—other people have noticed it too—military patrols on the streets. Frau Stühler also knows what the patrols were for. The army has been confined to barracks, from today the police also, no policeman is allowed to sleep outside the barracks anymore. There is so much desertion from the Volkstürm here and from the Eastern front. They are looking for fugitives, making checks. Yesterday, Frau Stühler divulged a curious fact: Order relayed to Aryan houses not to give bread to begging soldiers, still less a bed, and to chase away any who were persistent. In Dresden alone, patrols were said to have arrested about 700 deserters. Everything has been prepared for the evacuation of Dresden.—The Aryans have been evacuated from Breslau, but the Jews have been left in the city—the number of deserters detained in Dresden now stands at 17,000. Two days ago it was 700.

9

The Destruction of Dresden

IN THE MORNING—*February 13, 1945:* Yesterday afternoon Neumark called me over. I had to help him deliver letters this morning. I was quite unsuspecting. The circular to be delivered stated that one has to present oneself at 3 Zeughaus Strasse early on Friday morning, wearing working clothes and with hand luggage, which would have to be carried for a considerable distance, and with provisions for two or three days' travel, without exception regarded as a death march. The most cruel separations are taking place: Frau Eisenmann and Schorschi stay here. Lisel, the eleven-year-old, who wears the star, has to leave with his father and Herbert. No allowance is made for old age or youth, nor for seventy nor for seven—what they mean by "capable of work" is quite incomprehensible. I had to inform Frau Stühler, who was more shocked than on the death of her husband. Then I went by tram, I was permitted to do so, to the Station and Strehlen quarter with a list of nine names. Simon, not yet fully dressed, maintained his composure while his normally sturdy wife almost collapsed. Frau Gaehde in Sedan Strasse, very much aged, eyes staring, protested wildly and vehemently: She would fight to the last against this order, she could not leave her ten-year-old grandson, her seventy-year-old husband [while] her son-in-law was a prisoner of war. Frau Kreisler-Weidlich, of whose hysteria I had been afraid, was not at home; relieved, I dropped the sheet in the mailbox. A Frau Grosse stood helplessly by the telephone. "My poor husband, he is ill, my poor husband." I finally got the necessary signature acknowledging receipt and left. Hardly had I shut the corridor door than I heard her weeping loudly. Even more pitiful was Frau Bitterwolf in Struve Strasse. Again another shabby house, I was vainly studying the list of names in the entrance hall when a blond, snub-nosed young woman with a pretty, well-looked-after little girl, perhaps four years old, appeared. Did a Frau Bitterwolf live here? She was Frau Bitterwolf. I had to give her an unpleasant message. She read the letter, several times, said quite helplessly, "What is to become of the child?" then signed silently with a pencil. Meanwhile the child pressed up against me, held out her teddy bear, and radiantly cheerful, declared, "My teddy, my teddy, look!" The woman went silently up the stairs with the child. Immediately afterward I heard her weeping loudly. The weeping did not stop. . . .

EARLY EVENING—*Toward 7:00 P.M.:* At Neumark's the whole office was crowded with those to be deported. I shook hands with Paul Lang, Rieger, Lewinsky—"You're coming too? No?" With that there was already a gulf between us. I went upstairs to the Eisenmanns for a moment, the whole family had assembled—extremely upset. I went to Waldmann, who remains here. He set forth the gloomiest hypothesis with very great certainty. Why are the Jewish children being taken as well? There are murderous intentions behind it. And we who are left behind, "We have nothing more than a reprieve of perhaps a week. Then we'll be fetched out of our beds at six o'clock in the morning. And we'll end up just like the others, pushed onto a siding."

LATE EVENING[21]—We sat down for coffee at about half past nine on Tuesday evening, very weary and depressed, because during the day, after all, I had been running around as the bearer of bad tidings, and in the evening Waldmann had assured me with very great certainty (from experience and remarks he had recently picked up) that those to be deported

---

[21]As recorded ten days later by Victor Klemperer, having reached the town of Piskowitz.

on Thursday were being sent to their deaths ("pushed onto a siding"), and that we who were left behind would be done away with in just the same way in a week's time.—Then a full-scale warning sounded. "If only they would smash everything up." We very soon hear the ever-deeper and louder humming of approaching squadrons, the light went out, an explosion nearby. Pause in which we caught our breath, we kneeled head down between the chairs, in some groups there was whimpering and weeping—approaching airplanes once again, deadly danger once again, explosions once again. I do not know how often it was repeated. Suddenly the cellar window on the back opposite the entrance burst open, and outside it was bright as day. Fires were blazing at Pirnaischer Platz, on Marschall Strasse, and somewhere on or over the Elbe. The ground was covered with broken glass. A terrible strong wind was blowing. Natural or a firestorm? Probably both. In the hallway and on the side facing the Elbe, windows blown in. We could see big fires on the other side of the Elbe, on Marschall Strasse.

It was after midnight—we came upstairs at eleven. I thought: Just sleep, we're alive, tonight we'll have peace and quiet, now just put your mind at rest! As she lay down Eva said: "Air-raid warning."—"I didn't hear anything."—"Definitely. It wasn't loud, they're going around with hand sirens, there's no electricity." We hurried downstairs. The street was bright as day and almost empty, fires were burning, the storm was blowing as before. As usual a steel-helmeted sentry in front of the [synagogue] wall, between the two Zeughaus Strasse houses [Jews' houses]. . . . We came to the entrance hall of No. 3. At that moment a big explosion nearby, I kneeled, pressing myself up against the wall, close to the courtyard door. When I looked up, Eva had disappeared. I thought she was in the cellar. It was quiet. I ran across the yard to our Jews' cellar [and] called out several times to Eva. No reply. Big explosions. Again the window in the wall opposite burst open, again it was bright as day, again water was pumped. Then an explosion at the window close to me. A group of Russians—where had they come from?—pushed out the door. I jumped over to them. I had the knapsack on my back, the gray bag with our manuscripts, and Eva's jewelry in my hand, I stumbled and fell. A Russian lifted me up. To the side there was a vaulting of a half-destroyed cellar. We crowded in. It was hot. The Russians ran on in some other direction, I with them. Now we stood in an open passageway, heads down, crowded together. Explosions, light as day. I had no thoughts, I was not even afraid, I was simply tremendously exhausted, I think I was expecting the end. Someone called out, "This way, Herr Klemperer!" In the demolished lavatory there stood Eisenmann senior, little Schorschi in his arms. "I don't know where my wife is."—"I don't know where my wife and the other children are."—"It's getting too hot, the wooden paneling is burning, over there, the hall of the Reich Bank Building." We ran into a hall, it was surrounded by flames, but looked solid. "We must get down to the Elbe, we'll get through." He ran down the slope with the child on his shoulders; the route went close to fires, but it had to be cooler at the top and easier to breathe. To right and left buildings were ablaze, the Bellevue and—probably—the Art Academy. Whenever the showers of sparks became too much for me on one side, I dodged to the other. Was Eva lost, had she been able to save herself, had I thought too little about her? In my hands I held the precious bag [with the manuscripts] and—also the small leather case with Eva's woolen things, how I managed to hold on to it during all the clambering about is a mystery to me. I saw a stream of people on the road by the Elbe, but I did not have the courage to go down.

Finally, probably at about seven, the Brühl Terrace—the terrace forbidden to the Jews—was by now somewhat empty. I walked past the shell of the still-burning Bellevue and came to the terrace wall. A number of people were sitting there. After a minute someone called out to me. Eva was sitting unharmed on her suitcase wearing her fur coat. We greeted each other very warmly and were completely indifferent to the loss of our belongings, and remain so even now. At the critical moment, someone had literally pulled Eva out of the entry hall of No. 3 Zeughaus Strasse and into the Aryan cellar, she had gotten out to the street through the cellar window, had seen both Nos. 1 and 3 completely alight, spent the rest of the night looking for me, had in addition observed the destruction of the Thamm building, thus all of our furniture [stored since the loss of the Klötzschen home] and partly sitting in a cellar under the Bellevue. Once, as she was searching, she had wanted to light a cigarette and had no matches; something was glowing on the ground, she wanted to use it—it was a burning corpse. On the whole, Eva had kept her head much better than I, observed much more calmly and gone her own way. Every time I think of the pile of rubble of Nos. 1 and 3 Zeughaus Strasse, I nevertheless also have the atavistic feeling, "Yahweh!" That is where the Dresden synagogue was burned to the ground [on *Kristallnacht,* 1938]. Above us, building after building was a burned-out ruin. Down here by the river where many people were moving along or resting on the ground, masses of the empty, rectangular cases of the stick incendiary bombs protruded from the churned-up earth. Fires were still burning in many of the buildings on the road above. At times, small, and no more than a bundle of clothes, the dead were scattered across our path. Crowds streamed unceasingly, past the corpses and smashed-up vehicles, up and down the Elbe, a silent agitated procession. Then we turned right toward the town again. I let Eva lead the way and do not know where. Every house a burned-out ruin, but often people outside on the street with household goods they had saved. Again and again fires still burning. No attempts to extinguish them. Eventually Eva and I reached the Albertinum. The upper stories of the big building were burned. The cast-iron queen reigned unharmed up above, and there was no damage to the solid range of cellars, real catacombs. Very late at night Witkowsky came excitedly up to me, "We are all being taken out of here to Meissen, to Klotzsche [an airbase]." . . .

NEXT MORNING—*February 14:* We sat for a long time, dawn broke. Then another truck was ready. Several wounded on stretchers were put on, then we, the healthy ones, were pushed between them and to the back. A bumpy drive past ruins and fires. I could not see much from my seat, but the complete destruction ceased on the other side of Albertplatz.

February 15: The first delight was the huge pot of noodle soup in the dormitory. I calmly took the spoon of an old man who had eaten before me. I ate three big bowls. Then we went to look for our people and soon found them in an identical room in an identical building.

February 16: The *Kamenzer Tageblatt* [Kamenz Daily Paper]: "Summary courts martial have been set up. Every weakening of resistance is punishable by death." I link that with the desertions during our last days in Dresden. *The brief items on Dresden are shameless. Nothing but the irreplaceable works of art, not a word about the 200,000 dead.*[22] [sic]

"One death a tragedy—a million deaths a statistic." This bit of so-called wisdom has been attributed to Josef Stalin. In 1997 the *Moscow Times* found no record of Stalin ever having written such a statement.

[22]These estimated death toll numbers are today considered official:

More than 500,000	Tokyo, Japan	U.S. B29 fire bombings
90,000 to 166,000	Hiroshima, Japan	One U.S. atom bomb
60,000 to 80,000	Nagasaki, Japan	One U.S. hydrogen bomb
50,000	Hamburg, Germany	British and U.S. fire bombings
20,000 to 35,000	Dresden, Germany	British and U.S. fire bombings

10

Return of the Natives

LAST DAY OF THE WAR: In May the decision of people like Victor and Eva to return home seemed not that difficult. In spite of Dresden's massive destruction and well aware that all of Saxony would be under Soviet control, Eva and Victor still considered this their beloved city. They had been on the run since February, ever since they left the Klotzsche Airbase at Meissen. Finding their way village by village and town by town, mostly on foot, not knowing how far the reach of Soviet forces would be before it all collapsed, the Klemperers joined the masses trekking west. The hope was always to reach the advancing American forces before the collapse. They were now in Bavaria, the village of Tyroller-Gruber. Their shelter: an abandoned District SS building. Their momentary companions: German refugees from Silesia who told of the terror being laid on them by the Russians.

> *May 4, 1945:* The swastika outside was just above our window—*was,* I say. I slept on the wedge-shaped pillow of the SS, and the picture of Hitler is burning in our stove; despite all momentary difficulties and inconveniences (to which the cold, the rain, and muddy roads contribute a great deal) it is a joy to be alive.

72

May 5: It has been impossible to find out anything reliable, we have been without electric current and therefore cut off since April 28, that is, for one week. At supper young Asam had the most recent gossip, a newspaper sheet with the title *Nachrichten* [News], a week old. It is published in German by the American army in the territory it has occupied, and had reached here from Aichach. The sheet reported on the "historic meeting" of American and Russian troops in Torgau [Saxony]. Now the Reich has been torn in two—on the handshake between American and Russian commanders. We no longer need fear any Gestapo or any bomb.

May 6: Thus far unchallenged here. No mayor, no Americans—thus far. The latest rumor—someone is always "said" to have heard such and such a thing on some radio somewhere: Germany has capitulated to Eisenhower, but is continuing to fight against Russia; Goebbels has shot himself and his family, Hitler has disappeared.

May 8: This is the eleventh day without light, presumably it did not fall victim to a thunderstorm on April 28, but to the fighting. Without radio and without any news at all. When and how shall we be able to get away from here and get to Dresden? How on earth can we even get to Aichach and what shall we find there? To obtain real help, I would have to reveal myself as a Jew. But I would want to do that only when I can definitely and immediately leave my present surroundings. But the feeling of gratitude is nevertheless still constantly present, and many hours of the day are again and again enjoyable. Bucolic hours, so to speak. In addition also close to the people and therefore instructive.

May 9: "Total capitulation with the surrender of all submarines and 'midget submarines' was signed yesterday, May 8 at 3:00 A.M., on the German side by Admiral Dönitz." Asam gave out the report as reliable radio news: "But the thing about the Russians wasn't true. It wasn't mentioned," added Asam. So he too had believed just a little bit in this war between the USA and Russia. The many airplanes that passed over us yesterday in groups of three, very low and slow, are said to have been transports. Subjectively, from our point of view, the characteristic thing about them is that we no longer look for cover, are no longer afraid and yet with every airplane remember our past fear. . . .

HOME TO DÖLZSCHEN: On May 8, the same day Germany capitulated, Soviet occupation troops entered Dresden. For some time they had been camped out just sixty-six miles east across the Neisse River from Görlitz. That Dresden was never fought over some saw as a good omen. The lessons of the hopeless Battle for Berlin had not been lost. Of course every large German city had experienced death and destruction from the air, but for perceived tragedy Dresden's destruction seemed to top them all. It was clear that all of Saxony would be under Soviet military occupation. That issue had been settled in faraway places—especially Tehran in Iran and Yalta in the Crimea.[23]

The Klemperers were now homeward bound, always with difficulties, often by cart, needing a permit to board a train, packed together with former slave-laborers, concentration camp survivors, and other foreigners who just wanted to return to their home countries. The German police and their American supervisors were suspicious—why would a German go east, into the hands of the Soviets? Fortunately Victor still had his identity card with the "J." As long as he could convince the officials that Eva, the "Aryan," was indeed his legal wife, with zigs and zags they would eventually come through to Dresden.

June 10, 1945: The day began gloomily enough. Tired and hungry we walked to the Neustädter station—nada! We went to the police station opposite. Very friendly reception and one correct and one false piece of information. You must go to Dölzschen immediately! I objected that it would take time before I could move into my house there. The officer grinned:

[23]The Tehran Conference, November 28–December 1, 1943, Churchill, Roosevelt and Stalin; the Yalta Conference, February 4–7, 1945, Churchill, Roosevelt, Stalin.

You've no idea how quickly that can sometimes happen! And in that he proved to be right. Although I was helped by the fact that Berger [the "Aryan" de facto owner] had fled. But as far as our hunger was concerned, we were told that we would be fed at the refugee camp on Glacis Strasse, but there the rooms were empty, with Russian sentries sleeping on the top floor. So was a camp, I think on Margrafen Strasse. There we found only an army hospital, but no food. Then, still hungry and after an impossible night, we walked right through all the destruction of the city center. In Theater Strasse there was supposed to be an inquiry office with information about residents and people who had been bombed out. It was closed. Then we struggled—the word is no exaggeration!—along to the Swiss Quarter: Frau Ahrens' house, the Windes' house destroyed, no news about them to be had. Finally we found the Glasers' building, it was a little damaged inside, but on the whole wonderfully preserved, with nothing but ruins all around. This was where the day turned into a fairy tale. Frau Glaser welcomed us with tears and kisses, she had thought us dead. Glaser himself was somewhat decrepit and listless. We were fed, we were able to rest. In the late afternoon we walked up to Dölzschen.

ACCOMMODATION: The older generation of Saxonians could still remember 1918 and the trauma after the German surrender. The Kaiser had resigned, and a weak government of Social Democrats was anything but effective. Also, it didn't help that the victors had designed a devastating peace treaty, at least in the minds of Germans. In the wake of a collapsed economy, hyperinflation, hunger, unemployment, and hopelessness seemed to rule the day. By 1920, a battle for the hearts and minds of the people was raging across Germany. Saxony was indeed a hotspot. Marxist ideology and the new National Socialist promises, with a large dose of anti-Semitism, were both aimed at "the workers." Indeed the workers were suffering. But it went beyond that. Inflation can also destroy an entire middle class, on which Dresden's success had long depended. Budding intellectuals often reached out to the view of economics and society as

described by Karl Marx. In those years, young Victor
Klemperer, veteran of the lost war with his new Iron Cross
and a doctor's degree in philology, no doubt was among
them. By 1933 his side was definitely on the run.

After 1945, when the winning Soviets forced their vision of
a workers' paradise on Dresden, the hapless citizens, even the
intellectuals, were not immune to the call. Over at the university, the Jews were long gone. Meanwhile other respected professors had sailed along under the Nazi banner. Hardly had
the university reopened when most made accommodation
with the newest opportunity, generally by joining the
Communist Party. The question arises: Was it because these
distinguished intellectuals yet displayed that peculiarly Saxon
trait of being "up-to-date" for the next opportunity? Or was it
because they too were ordinary human beings who simply
wanted to get their own lives back in order?

In 1945, the Soviet occupation certainly was no picnic.
The victors were robbing their victims of anything and everything that even *looked* technological and could be moved—
bathroom fixtures, electrical equipment, pipelines, copper
wire, cook stoves, radios, also the tools of production—whatever the victors thought would be useful in their own war-
destroyed land. To the victor go the spoils, and there was no
doubt as to who the victor was in what later would be called
East Germany.

Having survived the National Socialists and the Dresden
firebombing, Victor and Eva Klemperer felt themselves
reborn. The last they had seen of their furniture, stored in a
warehouse, was the fireball consuming the entire building.
By that time they already considered themselves reasonably
safe on the Brühl Terrace above the Elbe. Wrote Victor at
the time, "of what importance is furniture anyway." At home
in Dölzschen, Eva was now busy with her garden, for it was
already June. The neurological problems that for years had
crippled her seemed to have disappeared entirely. Victor
joined the Communist Party and was back on the staff at the

Dresden University. By and by he was appointed professor at three other universities—Greifswald, Berlin, and Halle, all in East Germany. The two manuscripts he tried to complete in the first years at the Jews' house were saved. Eva, the "Aryan," had smuggled them to a friend in a nearby town before the Final Inventory was taken. These he retrieved and finished. Eventually, they were both published—an entire volume on Voltaire as well as one on Rousseau—proudly demonstrating Victor's passion for the French Enlightenment.[24] Even Victor's curious book on Nazi language was published.[25] All were reasonably successful during his lifetime, at least among his academic colleagues.

Eva Klemperer died in 1950, her various ailments having finally caught up with her. Two years later Victor Klemperer remarried. He died in 1960, at seventy-nine. Dr. Hadwig Klemperer, his second wife and widow, deciphered the entire handwritten text of the diaries, much of it having been written after the confiscation of Victor's typewriter. She then prepared the complete typescript, continuing Victor's determination to tell the entire tale. *I Will Bear Witness. 1933-1945,* in two volumes, was first published in German, in 1995. It became an instant sensation. The first English edition appeared in 1998, also to rave reviews.[26]

---

[24]*History of French Literature in the 18th Century,* Vol. I Voltaire; Vol. II Rousseau.

[25]*LTI - Lingua Tertii Imperii: Notizbuch eines Philologen, 1947I* [The Language of the Third Reich: A Philologist's Notebook]. Klemperer analyzes the way Nazi propaganda altered the German language, inculcating people with National Socialist ideas. Written from personal notes in his diary, beginning in 1933, and even more after 1935, it describes how a new language came to be naturally spoken by most of the population.

[26]Refer back to footnote 20.

Dresden Resurrected

11

How It All Happened

STALIN WINS: Begin with the Tehran Conference, November 1943: Germany's war was already into its fifth year. At first all had gone amazingly well, even after the initial invasion of Russia and the entry of the Japanese and Americans into the fray. For Germany, the added Pacific war had seemed little more than a distraction, especially while Japan was winning, island by island. On the eastern front, however, those early victories had already become history.

By November the tide in the Pacific began to turn. For the first time, American forces had retaken Guadalcanal, one of the Solomon Islands so easily captured by the Japanese months earlier. Likewise in the African Desert, with the help of U.S. supplies and troops, the British had stopped Germany's invincible General Rommel at El Alamein, Egypt. It had been a lengthy battle, weeks turning into months, finally ending in the defeat of Rommel's forces. British Prime Minister Winston Churchill is quoted as saying: "Before Alamein we never had a victory. After Alamein we never had a defeat."

Above all, the Battle for Stalingrad[27] was near closure. It had been raging since August. Afterward it was judged the bloodiest and perhaps the cruelest military battle of the Second World War. Combined military deaths on both sides exceeded two million. When it was all over, Stalingrad was in the hands of the Soviet armies. For Germany, as for the Soviet Union, this was the turning point of the war.

Time for the British and the Americans—already well acquainted—to meet with Soviet Russia at the top level, and so it was arranged. Between November 28 and December 1, Franklin Roosevelt, Winston Churchill, and Josef Stalin sat down at the Soviet Embassy in Tehran. The initial gathering was called for 6:00 P.M. on the twenty-eighth. Stalin arrived early, clearly flushed with the Stalingrad outcome. Roosevelt arrived precisely on time, brought into the hall in his wheelchair. As his aides would later report, the president was exhausted, having arrived a few hours earlier after a 7,000-mile flight. Winston Churchill strolled in an hour late. The following day the conference would begin in earnest.

Unfortunately the first dinner meeting got off to a bad start. According to U.S. notes, Stalin continuously needled Churchill about his perceived "affection" for the Germans. He proposed executing 50,000–100,000 German staff officers. Roosevelt joked that perhaps 49,000 would do. Churchill denounced the idea of "the cold blooded execution of soldiers who fought for their country." He said that "war criminals must pay for their crimes, and individuals who had committed barbarous acts . . . must stand trial at the places where the crimes were committed." He objected vigorously, however, to executions for political purposes. He even declared he would rather be taken outside and shot than agree to Stalin's proposal of summary executions for German officers. He stood up as if to storm out of the room.

[27]Later the city reassumed its historical name, Volgograd.

Stalin rose and intercepted Churchill, bringing him back to the table while assuring him he had only spoken in jest.

This shadow over the conference was not relieved by the deliberations that followed. For months Stalin had been pushing the western allies to open a second front. Churchill preferred an invasion from the Mediterranean Sea while Roosevelt promoted southern France from the Atlantic. Each had his reasons. In the discussion, the two western allies appeared to be bickering, which played well into Stalin's hands. Roosevelt prevailed and gave Stalin the promise that by May the western alliance would open a second front from the Atlantic. Stalin was satisfied. However, he was adamant in making permanent the 1939 partition of Poland between the Germans and the Soviets. The treaty was negotiated on the eve of the German invasion of Poland. The others went along with that, even agreed that the Oder-Neisse rivers would be a good demarcation between Germany and Poland, compensating Poland for its perceived loss of land.

Several other issues were also resolved, including commitment by Stalin for free elections in Poland. With that they agreed to meet again from time to time. As it turned out, "from time to time" was more than a year later. Soviet forces had already swept through the part of Germany east of the Oder and Neisse rivers and were just forty miles from Berlin. Stalin had insisted on having the conference somewhere in the Soviet Union, claiming his health prevented him from traveling abroad.

Hence the selection of Lavadia near Yalta in the Soviet Crimea, now a part of Ukraine. Completed in 1911 as a summer residence for Czar Nicholas and his family, the Lavadia palace incorporated the czarina's love for Italian Renaissance architecture. One might contemplate just how many summers the royal family spent at Lavadia, given the events of 1914 through 1917, after which all in the czar's

family were dead. At the time of this august gathering—
Churchill, Roosevelt, and Stalin—the palace was Stalin's summer residence. This would indeed be Stalin's conference,
and he would control the agenda. In history it is referred to
as the Yalta Conference.

Roosevelt presented a very different demeanor compared
to the meeting little more than a year ago. Every move now
was difficult; he occasionally seemed not to be paying attention. Still he came with an agenda: namely, to ensure Soviet
participation in the United Nations charter, which was moving
along nicely. Churchill was focused on securing free elections
for Soviet-liberated countries in eastern Europe. Roosevelt
was already distancing himself from his old wartime partner.
Churchill's presence seemed to be of no account. Stalin was
intent on building a Soviet sphere of influence in eastern
Europe. He appeared to go along with the idea of free elections as long as there was no outside supervision. His major
concern was making permanent the acquisition of eastern
Poland under the 1939 agreement with Hitler. He spoke at
length about this. Churchill fumed, and Roosevelt blunted any
criticism he might have had. Clearly the American president
was already fading when critical issues demanded the most
from him. Altogether the Yalta agreement strengthened com-
mitments already made at Tehran and assured Stalin's control
over postwar eastern Europe.

Almost as an afterthought, the Big Three discussed the issue
of governing Germany now that the invasion from both east
and west had reached the heartland. The agreement
included three zones of occupation—one for each of the
major allies—with details to be left for a future time. The
Soviets demanded Berlin, which lay inside the zone selected
for Soviet occupation. Still, Stalin agreed to separate occupation sectors within Berlin. When the question of a zone for
the French came up, Stalin said that too was okay with him

as long as the pieces for the French were taken out of the American and British zones and Berlin sectors.

The Land of Saxony was a piece of the Soviet zone as defined by the Big Three. It should have been no surprise when on May 8, 1945, the Russians and their armies simply moved into Dresden and took over what was left of the city. Now well-experienced in setting up Soviet-style provisional governments in eastern Europe, the military and the commissars proceeded with the task of constructing a Marxist enterprise in their occupation zones.

Less than a year later, Winston Churchill, by then the *former* British prime minister, would put the situation into a very few words, two of which so far have lived on in history:

> From Stettin in the Baltic to Trieste in the Adriatic an iron curtain has descended across the Continent.[28]

DDR *(DEUTSCHE DEMOKRATISCHE REPUBLIK):* In 1949 the occupation of Saxony and all areas of East Germany presumably came to an end. With a little help from the occupiers, the citizens of East Germany adopted a constitution and became a nation, almost. The one-time occupiers were now advisors, allies, and protectors. The constitution that created the DDR *mirrored* the Soviet model. Presumably the physical rebuilding of Dresden could now begin in earnest. That same year the area of West Germany adopted a constitution in line with the western democracies—the *Federal Republic of Germany (BRD).* Again, the occupiers became advisors, allies, and protectors. But in practice the DDR was quite another story.

By 1953 West Germany was rapidly rising out of the war's devastation, thanks to positive leadership and a highly moti-

---

[28]From a speech given March 5, 1946, at Westminster College in Fulton, Missouri.

vated population, not to mention substantial U.S. help from the Marshall Plan.[29] The extraordinary speed of recovery in the Federal Republic of Germany gave birth to a new expression—*Wirtschaftswunder* [economic miracle].

In the German Democratic Republic, however, the bloom of recovery had not yet shown its face. This was a Marxist state. The Soviet occupation never really ended. The leaders, generally elected in sham elections, were indeed Soviet puppets; the DDR had become just another Soviet satellite. Their protectors had found it in their own interest to decline Marshall Plan aid. At the same time, the DDR government was rapidly taking over all private sector manufacturing and commerce, in other words, attempting to build a classic Marxist paradise by seizing the means of production. The economy was in shambles and much of the population was angry. In the minds of the citizens, it was time to stand up.

The unlikely trigger of this brief uprising was pulled on June 16. According to the East German government, the rebuilding of Berlin's east (DDR) sector was not proceeding fast enough. Construction workers were ordered to increase production by ten percent, with no change in pay. The following day the workers went on strike. News spread quickly, and by late afternoon hundreds, perhaps thousands, of East Berlin citizens were pouring into the streets in support of the strikers.

East Germany's Soviet protectors immediately took action. The strike must be diffused, but the cat was out of the bag. Overnight word had spread from Berlin to the other East German states, above all to Saxony. A general strike was scheduled for the next day. In the major cities, Soviet troops

[29]The European Recovery Program (ERP) was the large-scale American program to aid Europe after the war. The plan was in operation for four years beginning in April 1948. The goals of the United States were to rebuild a war-devastated region, remove trade barriers, modernize industry, and make Europe prosperous again. The initiative was named after Secretary of State George Marshall.

and tanks were already on the streets. A photo from the time features a huge Soviet tank in the center of Leipzig, a crowd of protestors retreating before it. One enthusiastic young Saxon appears prepared to hurl a rock at the monster. It wasn't enough. That day across the land, hundreds were killed by the East German *Volkspolizei* and the Soviet military. The uprising had been quashed. The people were no match for their so-called protectors. The "next opportunity" would have to wait thirty-six years for another trigger that would break open the yoke laid on these old Saxons. And along the way it would become even worse before it began to get better.

THE BERLIN WALL: Clearly things were not going well in East Germany. In addition to the government's financial issues, there was an increasing epidemic of "brain drain." The best educated in science and innovative technology, the best in many intellectual fields were simply leaving the DDR for better opportunities as well as for freedom. It wasn't that easy to leave, for one must take the family along—otherwise severe reprisals—and leave with little more than the clothes on one's back. The preferred way was through Berlin, where the governing powers of the four sectors kept a minimum of communication open and where the streetcar rail system had been rebuilt and was running on time through the city. One could expect to escape with family and no real luggage as if on the way to a day at the beach on one of West Berlin's vacation lakes. It wasn't that easy, but it could be done without real danger. By 1961, sixteen years after the "iron curtain" came down, 1.65 million Germans had successfully made the leap. By and by, the East German government, especially its hard-line leader Walter Ulbricht, decided it had had enough of the escapees.

Over in Brussells one Uwe Siemon-Netto, writing for a major western newspaper, was biding his time in a hotel. Fifty years later he would write about how it was when the wall was built. Early on a Sunday morning, the phone rang.

It was his boss: "Uwe, you are going to Berlin. Ulbricht is building a wall."

That was on August 13, 1961. My longest working day ever lay ahead of me—36 hours. I took a Pan Am DC-6 to Tempelhof Airport in West Berlin and then drove in a rented car to Bernauer Strasse, a street dividing the French and Soviet sectors. On the eastern side, people roped themselves down from windows, while Communist cops stormed their apartment buildings from the backyard. Some refugees jumped into safety nets spread out for them by Western firemen. Nine days later, Ida Siekmann missed the net and dropped [to her death] on the sidewalk, becoming the first casualty of the Berlin Wall. For the next three months Bernauer Strasse became my most important place of work. I was there when East German workmen unrolled bales of barbed wire and later replaced the wire with a wall; when they rendered the Protestant Church of Reconciliation inaccessible; when workers' militiamen opened fire on a fugitive family of nine prompting a French lieutenant to blast off warning shots into the air from a machine gun mounted on his jeep: "Stop shooting or I'll aim my gun at you," he warned.

To my knowledge these were the only shots fired by an allied soldier in the 1961 Berlin crisis. The refugees made it safely across the border. . . . So, in 1961 U.S. President Kennedy did not interfere with the Communists as they walled in their own people. His stance would toughen significantly later under the influence of U.S. General Lucius D. Clay— "father of the Berlin airlift," whom Kennedy sent to Berlin as his personal representative. In 1963 Clay accompanied Kennedy on his trip to Berlin where JFK made his celebrated *"Ich bin ein Berliner"* speech. To this day, Clay is more beloved in Berlin than any other statesman of any nationality before and after him.[30]

VISITORS FROM ABROAD: In 1970, when Germans were first allowed to visit Poland, Michael Ripke with his mother Raba and his sister Katrina, plus three small children in a

---

[30]Siemon-Netto, Uwe, *The Washington Times,* August 15, 2011.

Volkswagen van, embarked on a mini-adventure—namely, to drive through East Germany, across the heavily controlled DDR landscape into Poland, all to visit the childhood home of Michael and Katrina. Until 1945 it was an idyllic childhood in Schreiberhau,[31] a ski resort in Germany, where their physician father was director of the only clinic. The idyll ended very suddenly in January 1945. Warnings were sent out that the Russians were near and no German military units were in the area. The entire town was preparing to flee west before the Russians arrived. Already they could hear the pounding of the large Soviet artillery. Father would stay, for he was the only physician in the town. Mother and three children—Michael, Katrina, and Thomas, a babe in arms—plus a nursemaid, together began the trek, first on foot to one town, having heard rumor a train was arriving, not so, then to another town—the train was overcrowded with wounded soldiers and civilians who had simply forced their way through the doors or windows. Finally the little troupe found a train, but that was only briefly, then by foot, in a horse car, overnight in a barn, on and on by foot, seemingly for days, until their arrival at Buch far to the northwest, a place designated earlier as a Kleist family gathering refuge.

Now twenty-five years later this little pilgrimage was to become another mini-adventure. In Poland they found Schreiberhau. It was perhaps what they expected—new people, new street names, and another language, certainly not the home of their childhood.

It was the trip back, however, that still causes a shudder. Why not drive through Dresden on their way home to Heidelberg. Expectations were not high, knowing the history of the firebombing and the nature of the DDR. When Michael realized they would never reach Dresden if they remained on the autobahn, he simply steered the van to a country road—forbidden of course. Winding through the

[31]Today, Szklarska Poręba in Poland.

countryside, they did eventually reach Dresden. As Michael now remembers—a city of large open spaces and huge blackened derelict monsters standing together. So this is what had once defined the legendary Old City of Dresden.

By chance, just three years later, Jane of the magic carpet group paid a solitary visit to Dresden. Why, she can't exactly remember, but it had to do with the legendary baroque Old City and the Zwinger Palace. The train from Frankfurt had been delayed at the border while the East German border patrol unloaded all the passenger coaches, one at a time, to inspect the contents of the hand-carried luggage. One can imagine this American innocent was a bit nervous. She ought not to have been. The guard quickly motioned her to close the cover, without inspection. Every other passenger in line—mostly women—appeared to be from West Germany. No doubt they were bringing clothing—sweaters, underwear, children's shoes, and baby clothes—to their relatives in the east. Every sweater and most of the baby clothes were confiscated, thrown behind the counter onto a large pile of beautiful hand-knit sweaters, mittens, and caps. The women watched in silence. No one complained out loud.

Not until dusk did the train arrive in Dresden. The train station had been somewhat restored after that fateful 1945 bombing, yet it stood alone and was dimly lit. No streetlights of any kind outside and apparently no buildings nearby. The traveler was directed to a wide exit from the station. The walk to her hotel would be about twenty minutes along a paved avenue—*the Prag Strasse.* So she was told. Thus she began her trek, dragging her bag on its four wheels. She noticed on both sides of the broad avenue tall, solid wooden walls, much taller than pedestrian height. Perhaps the spaces behind held building materials, for by this time Dresden was slowly putting itself back together in the outer neighborhoods. The traveler was not frightened. She knew this was a Communist country. Any vagrants, thieves, kidnappers, or murderers surely were under lock and key, if not under the sod. This comforted her. Eventually a tiny light became visible at the far end of the tunnel. Coming closer it revealed a small hotel—possibly a restored and remodeled orphanage building, for the corner of the street was labeled *Waisenhaus Strasse* [Orphanage Street]. The East German travel bureau in Berlin had referred to it as a former boys' school. Whatever its history, the exhausted traveler had finally found a blessed retreat.

The following morning in the breakfast room, she noticed a group of German men, perhaps in their forties. One could not help but notice them, for they were engaged in boisterous and good-natured conversation. They invited the visiting American to join them. She demurred. Yet the friendly encounter quickly endeared the entire group to her. The men turned out to be a delegation of engineers from Leipzig, in Dresden to help design a street system for modern times. These few highway planners could have been her colleagues at Honeywell—engineers out on a business junket and filled with enthusiasm for the work ahead. Can it be that among the people of Germany, the Saxons are most like midwestern Americans?

That morning the traveler left the hotel with a smile, having received walking directions to the fabeled *Zwinger.* Her destination—the Old City, once the site of baroque architectural treasures among a forest of other treasures as well. Decades earlier there were many, then there were none, and now there was one. So she understood.

In thirty minutes, along a somewhat-traveled avenue, she came upon a baroque wonder, apparently set out on a broad plain, surrounded by nothing. So this was the resurrected Zwinger, the great wall pavilion whose baroque arms once stretched a hundred meters in both directions. In the visitor's mind, this centerpiece of balanced beauty was only enhanced by its loneliness. She wanted to weep, but then she noticed groups of small bricks here and there nearby, even a bit farther away. So carefully were the bricks piled, so pur-

posely placed in small groups, one could imagine each brick
patiently awaiting its resurrection as a small part in two
reconstructed arms that would once again reach out from the
jeweled pavilion.

Yet the visitor neither understood the larger picture nor
attempted to walk farther toward the Elbe River. There she
would have found an entire city of ruins. Over two centuries,
a large part of the Dresden population had lived there and
still did. She would later learn that at this time it was a bit of
a mismatch. Some of the older housing had been repaired,
but most of the residential buildings had been destroyed in
the firebombing. These were being replaced with modern
Soviet-style multifamily edifices. In between these forgettable
structures stood the silent ruins of one or another once-trea-
sured edifice—from baroque to late nineteenth century. After
the war, the people of Dresden had voted overwhelmingly to
restore their Old City. Yet never was there enough money
on hand in East Germany. Never could a timeline be set. So
beloved was the earlier memory that the population was willing to wait.

Those once enamored with the dream of a Marxist paradise needed only to look across the border at their cousins
in the west. In Dresden, the Marxist dream was gradually
dying as the realization solidified. In spite of excellent edu-
cation, in spite of efforts to rebuild Dresden as an innovative
technology center for the future, in spite of plans upon plans
to rebuild the Old City, it was the *System* that couldn't
deliver.

Except for the exquisite Zwinger pavilion, the walk to the
Old City evoked little more than sadness. Still the visitor had
one more assignment in Dresden. Marianne Hauptmann, a
friend from home, originally from Dresden, had asked a
favor of her. In January 1933, Marianne, from a Jewish family, had finished her law studies at the Dresden University. In
her graduating class was a good friend who was not Jewish.
She promptly received her license to practice the law.

Unexpectedly one of the very first laws passed by the new Nazi government prohibited Jews from becoming licensed. At that moment Marianne's law career was finished even though it hadn't even begun. For a time she found some kind of paralegal work until that too was forbidden. Fortunately Marianne lived at home with her widowed mother. After the Nazi takeover, her brother, who had been an active Communist, immediately went underground. One way or another, probably through Portugal, he found his way to Bolivia and even married there. Marianne's sister Helga was already married. She and her husband stuck it out in Dresden for a couple more years, then managed a visa to China. There they would spend the war years interned by the Japanese military government. Both survived.

Marianne stayed at home until it was almost too late. In early 1939, she finally received a visa to Great Britain. Surely with great regret she left her mother alone and joined the long line of refugees. Before leaving, Marianne asked her law school friend to look after her mother the best she could and to rescue any of her mother's belongings if she should be evacuated. After the war, this friend was still living in the family home, somewhat damaged in the war but beyond the area of the firebombing. Yes, she had tried to help Frau Hauptmann, but after the yellow strip was placed across the Hauptmann apartment, there was nothing more she could do. Frau Hauptmann's evacuation was imminent. And her household property was now the property of the government. It would soon be auctioned off. Frau Hauptmann nevertheless dared give to Marianne's friend her porcelain Meissen vanity set. As long as her children could remember, it had always graced their mother's dresser. The friend agreed to keep it until Frau Hauptmann returned. Of course, Frau Hauptmann never returned, nor did Marianne. After the war, she and her siblings were reunited in Minneapolis, and the two law school friends reconnected through letter exchanges. The exchange ceased once the Cold War was in full bloom. Marianne claimed to understand, for this Dresden friend was now a judge in the District Family Court. In East Germany, correspondence with the enemy was more than suspect.

When, in 1973, Marianne learned that her friend Jane would be visiting Dresden, she met with her to ask a favor. And so it was on the afternoon of Jane's visit to Dresden that she hired a taxi to take her to the home of Marianne's friend, the judge. At one time it undoubtedly had been an elegant neighborhood with deep setbacks from the street and groves of trees protecting against the traffic noise. Stucco and stone were the style. Obviously the elements had taken their toll. But within the possibilities available, this was still a neighborhood that held its head high.

The visitor ventured up the stone walk. The front door was already open. The judge warmly welcomed Marianne's American friend. Inside, the living room furnishings reflected a proper German home, with a coffee table already set for the visitor. Forty years later this American visitor has forgotten much of what was said. However, she does remember what was important. First of all, the judge claimed to despise the government and the system under which her land was forced to live. Fortunately, as a family court judge, she dealt with family issues, much like a social worker. Politics did not play much of a role. That having been said, Marianne's friend continued with some agitation. She had a sister living in West Germany who visited from time to time. She had Dresden friends whose families from West Germany also visited occasionally. The judge resented very much the superior attitude of these relatives whose lives had become so successful and whose cities were becoming so beautiful. It was as if the people of Dresden were responsible for their fate. The judge informed the visitor that the Russians had stolen from their city everything left of any value. Furthermore, East Germany had been denied the Marshall Plan aid that underwrote the remarkable recovery on the west side. As a counterpoint to her argument, she indicated she looked forward to retirement. After retirement, travel to the west was not difficult. If the traveler did not wish to return from such a marvelous land, her government would not mind at all—one less pension to pay.

When it was time for the American visitor to move on, her hostess went to the sideboard and picked up a small piece of Meissen porcelain. This, she explained, was the pin dish belonging to the Hauptmann vanity set. Making no mention of the other, larger pieces, she rather gingerly wrapped the small piece in tissue paper. Would the visitor kindly deliver it to their mutual friend Marianne? Of course. The visitor left and hailed a taxi, for it was getting dark. The following morning she would be leaving by train for Berlin.

Two weeks later, at home, Jane called on Marianne. She described her visit with the judge and presented to this friend the little package. Marianne carefully unwrapped it and proceeded to examine the small porcelain pin dish. Nodding a bit, she declared: "Yes, this is my mother's porcelain. Thank you for bringing it to me." That was all. On a number of occasions afterward, Jane spent time with Marianne and her sister Helga in their home. Never was a word said about the Meissen porcelain or the beautiful vanity set that had once belonged to their mother.

12

Die Wende (The Change)

It happened so suddenly the import can almost be missed. It should have happened years ago. It should never have had to happen. So be it. What was casually agreed to back at Tehran and Yalta had consequences that even today have ramifications. Where did the change begin? Some say in the Soviet Union, where change also was long past due. In 1985 Mikhail Gorbachev became premier of a troubled empire. Over in Poland, what began as an ordinary shipyard strike was rapidly devouring the government. Estonia and Lithuania, both a piece of the Soviet system, had declared their independence. Gorbachev tried to stem the flow by restructuring production and distribution. He called it *perestroika.* He also allowed public criticism of the ruling communist party—*glasnost.* It was too little and too late. The Czech Republic opened its gates to Hungary and Hungary opened its gates to Austria. Within months—nay, weeks—everywhere the Iron Curtain was disintegrating. In East Germany, the government was promising this and promising that. Could the system still hold on? For Premier Erik Honecker and his crowd it would also be too late.

MONDAY DEMONSTRATIONS: It had all begun in Saxony, land of those hearty Leipzig engineers. It was Monday evening, September 4, following the weekly prayer service for peace at the Nikolai Church in Leipzig. After the service, the worshipers flowed out of the church and gathered in the courtyard. Something was in the air, and those Saxon opportunists could sense it. Expanding on words of Martin Hüneke: "*We Saxons are ahead of the curve.*" In 1989 they certainly had it right. Yet even today, because of their dialect and enthusiastic approach to life, outsiders often regard the people of Saxony as a bit simple-minded. "How wrong these critics are!" So says Martin Hüneke.

Others soon joined the demonstrations, knowing that this particular church had a reputation as a center of peaceful resistance. Their demands were simple: Allow the citizens of East Germany to travel freely abroad and to elect their government democratically. Once news of the gathering spread across the land, other cities and towns picked up the cry. Every Monday now begat a *Monday March* in East Germany, with hundreds, sometimes thousands, gathered in city squares, all united in peaceful opposition to the regime. The chant alone had spunk—"We are the people" *[Wir sind das Volk]*.

Throughout September thousands of East German citizens, who also sensed an opportunity brewing, were finding their way to the German Embassy in Prague. The hope was to gain permission for travel by train to West Germany. Normally impossible with East Germany in between. Yet the situation was critical, for the embassy had no way of accommodating so many refugees. The West German government negotiated an agreement with their Marxist cousins whereby these refugees were permitted to travel through East Germany unmolested by East German authorities. On October 3, when a convoy of sealed passenger trains paused in the Dresden station, the East German military did not molest them. However, chaos almost erupted as more East Germans attempted to jump on. The police pulled them off.

In Leipzig, those few who had gathered at the Nikolai Church on September 4 had grown to 120,000 two weeks later. Obviously these gutsy Saxons, together with their children and grandchildren, had correctly sensed this "next opportunity." Back in Berlin, the Politburo was in shambles. General Secretary Erich Honecker was forced to resign. Others soon followed, and by the first week of November the entire Politburo as well as the East German cabinet had resigned. The new government announced East Germans would be permitted to cross the border into the west at will.

On November 9, the Berlin wall was breached from both sides, with eager young people, chisels and hammers in hand, leading the attack. Soldiers and police on the east side stood back. Some even joined the crowd. One by one, the heavily guarded checkpoints were opened. Berlin was now a single city. On March 18, the first free elections in fifty-eight years were held. By July 1, the entire Berlin Wall was history. Likewise, slowly but surely the thousand-mile "wall" of electric fences, no-man's-land, and guard towers encircling East Germany were dismantled. A massive exodus of East Germans flooded across what was once a deadly border. The influx of these new "refugees" created its own issues, but somehow the German penchant for organization even managed this.

On October 3 of 1990, the newly elected governing body of what was once East Germany voted to join the *Bundesrepublic.* Germany was democratically reunited.

THE UNFOLDING: In the midst of all this excitement, Helen Kuehn, who much later participated in two of the "Missions" and most recently was a piece of the magic carpet foursome, arrived in Dresden on a bus tour of curious Americans. They wanted to see for themselves the fabled City of

Dresden, now liberated. Helen had an additional mission of her own. Back in 1935, when she was a small child, her Aunt Helen Kuehn had sent Helen a picture postcard from Dresden—the elegant Bellevue Hotel where she was staying. On the back, Aunt Helen wrote about the beautiful view of the Elbe River from her hotel room. As a child, Helen had often dreamed of seeing Dresden through a window of the elegant Bellevue. As it turned out, the 1990 group did not stay at the Bellevue. Perhaps it too was under reconstruction.

The guided tour of the Old City was anything but forget-table—the royal castle and a dozen other baroque survivors were covered with scaffolding while busy workers every-where were pushing, pulling, hammering, and drilling, as if to make up for forty-five years of lost time. Truly, there was something schizophrenic about the place. Amid the rising structures, giant hulks of stone and iron—the skeletons of other treasures—stood by silently, no doubt each awaiting its own resurrection.

Was it possible that the people of Dresden would some-day make a lie of the lament the great German author and poet Erich Kästner wrote in 1945 on first seeing his child-hood home?

> I was born in the most beautiful city in the world. Even if your father, my child, was the richest man in the world, he could not take you to see it, because it no longer exists. . . . In a thousand years was her beauty built, in one night was it utterly destroyed.

A TALE OF TWO CASTLES: This is the day the travelers have long anticipated. Already the decision has been made. It will be a taxi day, for they are all strangers to the traffic patterns as well as the parking options. The Volvo will stay home while they are out and about. As they make their way by taxi, they note the broad streets with a minimum of congestion, quite unlike Berlin and Szczecin. It must be that four decades ago those enthusiastic Saxon engineers designed a traffic system for Dresden that was even better than "up-to-date."

They engage the taxi driver in a short conversation. Before the *Wende*—that euphemistic name for the fall of Communism in Germany—the driver was a bureaucrat in the government system. He also reminds them there was never any unemployment in East Germany. After the *Wende* and the virtual destruction of the government system, each employee was given five years to find new employment, perhaps a new career. He tried, but it was impossible. Still, the driver acknowledged, "In the new system everything else is much better." Thanking him for this bit of insight, the travelers pay a decent tip and are on the way by foot.

In fact, they are right at a portal of the Zwinger, that baroque beauty dreamed up by the eighteenth-century ruler, Augustus I, Prince Elector [*Kürfurst*] of Saxony. The word *Zwinger* apparently refers to a royal space between a pair of wall fortifications. If there ever was a pair, one of them seems to have disappeared long ago. The original Zwinger Wall Pavilion backs up to the remnant of the remaining wall.

Already the morning crowds have arrived. The elegant, exquisite square about which the galleries and pavilions of the prince's palace are ringed is already crowded with visitors, for this is the start of the annual *Wende* holiday, remembering October 3, 1990. The visitors don't meander too far from one another. Still, each one has a different take on the historic beauties. Jane is scrounging in her memory, trying to recall her Zwinger encounter back in 1973. This portal must have been the lonely pavilion that stood on an empty plain in that earlier time. Now surrounded by galleries left and right leading to crowned arches, more galleries, and the great renowned Masters Gallery, it is just one beautiful part of a baroque puzzle whose pieces fit perfectly together.

Augustus I, the instigator of this wonder, is worth a word here. He ascended the Saxon throne in 1694, well after the wars of the Protestant Reformation had been settled one way or another. Among the German principalities and kingdoms, "settled" meant being either Protestant or Catholic. Inasmuch as Martin Luther, whose ninety-five theses posted on a church door had lit the fire of the Reformation, it is not surprising to learn he was born in Saxony, reared in Saxony, and taught in Saxony. Might one trace in this act of defiance an outcropping of those Saxon traits?

In German lands these were times of relative peace and prosperity. As a reflection of his eminence, Prince Augustus I named Dresden his Royal City, then went off to France and Italy to take in the architectural wonders so described. Why not a Versailles for Dresden? Such were the beginnings of the Zwinger, the Royal Castle, and the Green Vault [*Grüne Gewölbe*], this last a storage place for Augustus's growing collection of world treasures. It is considered part of the new Albertinum, home to one of the greatest of European art collections. One might thank the princes Augustus I and II for such a holding. In the late nineteenth century, a nearby armory was extended and converted into the Albertinum, a museum for modern art. Like most of the Old City, the building was bombed and burned in the great firebombing. Victor Klemperer referred to this in his diary, for it is the place to which he and Eva fled from the Brühl Terrace. The upper stories had been burned and destroyed. Underneath were the "cellars and catacombs," where they spent the night with others and from which they were all fetched by trucks and taken out of the city. The Albertinum was one of the earliest buildings to be restored, reopening in 1953. Tragedy struck again in 2002 when the entire Old City was covered by a hundred-year-high Elbe flood, fatally weakening the foundations of the Albertinum. This time the old building just didn't make it. It was brought down and then rebuilt nearby in a manner sympathetic to this reborn baroque city.

More than three centuries after Augustus I, these treasures have not been equaled elsewhere. But for Augustus this was not quite enough. On learning that an opportunity was at hand to be *king* of the great but weakened Polish-Lithuanian

Empire, he stepped up. He would have to be elected by the Polish parliament, which took a bit of money and influence. Apparently Augustus had enough of both. Still needed, however, was a Catholic king, for Poland was indeed a Catholic nation. Quite a step for this ruler whose subjects had fought and died to preserve a Protestant land in the mold of Martin Luther. Augustus I not only converted to Catholicism, but he brought his young son along also, then ordered construction of a Catholic cathedral next to the Royal Castle in Dresden. And so it was done.

In 1697, Prince Augustus I of Saxony was elected King Augustus II of Poland, which included rights to an ancient castle in Warsaw. Standing at the gate of Warsaw's original Old Town, it had been the royal castle of the Polish kings since 1526. Over the years, it had been partially destroyed, looted, repaired, and always rebuilt by subsequent rulers. Augustus made a number of additions and improvements to the castle. After his death in 1733, his son King Augustus III inherited the castle and all that went with it. He died in Warsaw and is buried there, but his heart is buried in the family crypt in Dresden. Thus ended the brief reign of the Saxon kings in Poland.

We already know the beginnings and the end of the royal castle in Dresden, the date: February 15, 1945. Before moving on too quickly, let us review the end of the ancient royal castle in Warsaw, which had occurred a few months earlier. This brings us back to the beginning of World War II and the German invasion of Poland, September 1939. It was all over by the end of the month. Germany had conquered Poland west of the line to which Hitler and Stalin had earlier agreed. The Soviet Union promptly took over the eastern part.

It seems Hitler's plan, no doubt supported by a cadre of believing experts, called for the total destruction of several major Polish cities, including Warsaw. In 1940, he favorably reviewed a plan devised by his "Chief Architect for

Warsaw," one Herr Pabst. Basically, Warsaw's 1.5 million citizens would be evacuated[32] one way or another from the city. Most areas and monuments would be destroyed and a new city of 130,000 Germans would be built. In place of the Warsaw castle, a large People's Party Hall would be constructed. That area, including Warsaw's Old Town, would also be eliminated, to be replaced by a major transportation hub. Responding to Hitler's enthusiasm, German forces drilled holes throughout the castle so that it might be dynamited to ensure complete destruction. The plan was not carried out, for Hitler's ally in Italy, Benito Mussolini, objected. Yet the initial invasion had already destroyed much of the Old Town and badly damaged the castle.

Almost four years later, August 1, 1944, the Warsaw Home Army[33]—40,000 strong—was encouraged by the exile government in London to rise up, promising airdrops of ammunition and other supplies. Likewise broadcasts from Moscow exhorted the Home Army that it was time to act. The western allies' airdrops turned out to be miniscule. Soviet forces on the east, who had already reached the Vistula River and Warsaw suburbs, were expected to attack as a diversion. It never happened for reasons known only to the Soviet High Command. After sixty-three days the uprising was thoroughly crushed. As punishment, Hitler ordered the castle, the entire Old Town, and much, much more to be destroyed by dynamite. This was promptly done immediately following the surrender of the Warsaw Home Army. The Soviet army did not advance into Warsaw until January 1945, after the German army had expelled more than a half million Poles from the city, to be disposed of one way or another.

---

[32]In the words of Nazi-speak, "evacuation" meant deportation to slave labor in Germany or a concentration camp. After 1942, the word in Nazi-speak was "deportation," which meant "to a death camp in Poland."

[33]An underground army of 40,000 well-organized fighters.

Fortunately history moved on, even behind the Iron Curtain. For Warsaw as for Dresden, this meant rebuilding plans of any kind required permission from Moscow. Royal castles probably sounded a bit bourgeois to Soviet bureaucrats. Nevertheless the population both in East Germany and in Poland clamored, and the messages did get through. In both cities, design and construction were initiated. And in both cities it was private donations from around the world that made it all happen. Though reconstruction of the Dresden royal castle began back in the 1970s, work is still ongoing in this twenty-first century. Yet the castle has been open for a number of years and no one seems to notice. People have learned to be patient. The Warsaw castle rebuilding began in 1980. Four years later, the castle opened for visitors. In 1986, Jane from our magic carpet foursome and her husband Arthur toured the castle. Most conspicuous was a pair of stunning identical large inlaid chests. They stood to the left and to the right as one entered the great entrance hall of the castle. Above each was a plaque in Polish and in German:

> Gift to the Polish people from the people of the German Democratic Republic[34]

> Gift to the Polish people from the people of the Federal Republic of Germany[35]

Surely those two early Saxon princes, Augustus I and Augustus II, would have been mighty pleased with these twin gestures of friendship.

OLD CITY/NEW CITY: Back to Dresden where the four visitors are rambling among open spaces and massive structures, of intricate design and pastel colors. Past the royal castle they

[34]*Deutsche Demokratische Republik.*

[35]*Bundesrepublik Deutschland.*

come upon an open square flanked on one side by the Catholic cathedral, on the other by the Semper Opera House, *Semperoper* in German. Though twice destroyed by fire in modern history, it has never lost its premier standing within the culture of European music. In 1869, the opera house was nearly burned down by accident. In the fire-bombing of 1945 it was totally destroyed. In 1985, on the fortieth anniversary of the destruction, the rebuilt opera house opened exactly as it was before the firestorm. One can only imagine the applause that night. Once again the great composers of opera—Richard Wagner, Richard Strauss, even Kurt Weill—resounded from the walls of the opera house. Since the *Wende,* the stage and the orchestra pit have been enlarged. Beginning in 2008, the annual opera ball has drawn two thousand attendees from far and wide, to waltz on the stage and in the orchestra pit below while hundreds more watch from the balconies above.

Today a trio of musicians is performing in a corner of the *Semperoperplatz.* They play very well, listenable tunes from here and there. Crowds are moving up and down to and from the plateau above. No one seems to be paying attention. One of the travelers stops to thank the musicians, in English, and to inquire whence they have come. "From St. Petersburg," one of the musicians volunteers. The visitors find a table and sit down to order coffee. Presently the musicians begin to play—of all things, "The Star Spangled Banner." Apparently Americans are easily spotted. No one turns a head, but the traveling foursome waves a bit and returns to put a Euro in the basket.

Later they pass by the *Frauenkirche,* whose fate has waxed and waned with the vagaries of history. When Augustus I of Saxony honored his religious conversion by building a Catholic cathedral next to the castle in this Protestant land, the good burghers of Dresden fought back in their own way. They would build the greatest church of all and dedicate it to the Virgin Mary. They were just as Christian as the Papists!

Somehow in Dresden private money could always be found. Remember, these Saxons were of up-and-coming stock. And so the church was completed in 1726, but without the magnificent dome. The artisans had claimed it was impossible to build. Eventually Prince Augustus I prevailed. The artisans then came around and built the tower. No wonder the prince is known in history as Augustus the Strong, bragging that he could break a horseshoe in half with his hands, even as he suffered greatly from ill health. In 1743, the Church of Our Lady *(Frauenkirche)*, with its 96-meter-high dome, was completed. The once-timid artisans had risen to the occasion. Mounted on a pedestal outside the church entrance is a large bronze cast of Martin Luther wearing his familiar pastor's robe. In his hand he holds the Bible, as if to say, "Let passersby forevermore know to whom this church belongs."

In 1945 when the *Frauenkirche* was totally destroyed in the firebombing, poor Martin Luther landed on the ground face down. But he did survive amid the rubble. The great cleanup turned out to be an effort of several years, much of the work done with shovel and wheelbarrow by the women of Dresden. Conspicuous in the Old City center is the statue of a woman in her apron pushing a wheelbarrow of rubble, dedicated of course to the women of Dresden. Yet no move was made to rebuild the church. Rather a "Warning Against War" was constructed by piling as much as possible of the *Frauenkirche* rubble on the spot where the church once stood. The rubble was flanked by two remaining partial walls. The population repeatedly let its wants of a resurrected church be known. The government continued to be unresponsive, perhaps because of cost, more likely out of fear that a heightened Christian awareness might seize the population. For behind the Iron Curtain, the City of Dresden was being hailed as a star in the world of successful Bolshevism.

Change cannot be boxed in forever, nor was it in the case of Dresden. In 1990, even before the magic October 3 *Wende,* a new nonprofit funding mechanism was formed:

The Organization of Support for the Resurrection of the *Frauenkirche*.[36] Funds flowed in from throughout the world, notably from West Germany, where feelings ran high and economic recovery was creating a largesse. Altogether private donations paid a third of the €129 million cost. The Federal Republic, the Land of Saxony, and the City of Dresden contributed the rest. Plans and excavations were already under way. By 2004, with Martin Luther back on his pedestal, Dresden and Saxony celebrated the resurrection of the Church of Our Lady. The church today is often considered the prime attraction in the Old City.

The traveling foursome is on its way to lunch at the Westin Bellevue, having discovered that it was reconstructed on the other side of the Elbe River. They pause briefly at the *Frauenkirche* to peer through the inside iron gates. The incredible nave, with angels large and small floating above and behind the altar, seems to take their breath away. Tonight two of the magic carpet foursome will attend Bach's B minor Mass in concert at the church. It is sold out, but they already have their tickets and have promised the sleepy-heads to report back on the morrow.

Now across the Elbe River on the Augustus Bridge, then a short walk along the strand to reach the hotel. It turns out to be more Westin than Bellevue. Exquisite in every detail, but not quite the same as Helen's 1935 treasured postcard. Today is Katrina's birthday. The four are alone in the dining lounge. Michael has ordered the wine. Before too long they shall be in Berlin, where Michael's sister Katrina awaits the reunion. A quick cell phone call and Katrina is on the line, warm good wishes from each of the Dresden four to the *Geburtstagskind* (birthday child), who is indeed a friend forever. Can you imagine, just twelve years ago on this day, they were together in a Szczecin hotel drinking a birthday toast to Katrina. Will it ever again happen this way?

[36] *Gesellschaft zur Förderung des Wiederaufbaus der Frauenkirche e.V.*

Three Americans dwarfed by the gate inside the Zwinger

Saturday Evening, Bach's B minor Mass in concert at the *Frauenkirche*

13

Ahead of the Curve

Back to the Saxons, whom the travelers met earlier. All sorts of traits have been attributed to them—enthusiastic, up-and-coming, the first on the block, and always on the lookout for new and creative ideas. During the years of inflation after the First World War, it seemed the Communists offered the best and the boldest of visions; a bit later, as the Great Depression unfolded, the Nazis pinpointed the blame and offered a quick solution. That one those Saxons and many others bought. But it turned out quite the opposite. As disaster after disaster after disaster unfolded, these good Saxons were simply upended and tried to accommodate. And then one day the Berlin Wall fell down. The new scent of freedom—of liberty—breathed life into all that too long had lain dormant. Innovation, creativity, and much more burst forth.

Through the centuries when times were ripe, these twin traits revealed themselves in spades. An example: In the eighteenth century, our old friend Prince Augustus I hired one Johann Bottger, an alchemist who made the mistake of boasting about his talents for "creating gold." So enthusiastic was the prince that he put the young man under house arrest in the expectation the poor fellow would create gold out of a lesser metal, just for him. Even after years of confinement the young man yet failed, but in the meantime he had created the magic formula for producing strong white translucent porcelain. So began Augustus's new fancy, the manufacture of the best porcelain in the world. The prince initially built a factory in Dresden. Later he expanded it to nearby Meissen. Finally, Johann Bottger was set free. Unfortunately, Augustus did not make much money on the venture, for the best of the pieces he put into his own treasury. These survived the firebombing quite well, having been removed for safekeeping. By the way, Meissen porcelain still claims to be the best.

1928: The rise and fall of Dresden's first *Kugelhaus* [spherical house]. During the brief prosperity of the late 1920s, the entrepreneurial citizens of Dresden seized an emerging opportunity. Promoting themselves as the "City of Technology," the citizens built an expansive multistory Municipal Exhibition Center in one of the city's green areas. Initially it was quite a success—exhibitions featuring the best of what German industries had to offer. But none of this drew as much attention as the centerpiece of the Center, *Das Kugelhaus,* and spherical it was, with a diameter of 24 meters and a height of 26.5 meters, including the ball neck on which it was mounted. Promoted as the first *Kugelhaus* ever built, it was wildly popular. The *Kugelhaus* showcased a number of emerging technologies, especially those demonstrating electrical engineering and new sources of energy. With five levels of showrooms, mounted on the inside periphery, and a Meissen Porcelain showroom on the ground floor, the entire interior was open as in an atrium. A popular restaurant was perched on the sixth floor, with a modern elevator providing the transportation.

The *Kugelhaus* frame was steel with an outside metallic skin of sheet aluminum, except for the windows circling the building at each level. These provided panoramic views of the entire city. When lit at night, the *Kugelhaus* presented a spectacular vision. But alas, by the mid-thirties when German commerce and industry were fully occupied with rearmament, the mood of the city and the nation had shifted dramatically. The death knell of the first-ever *Kugelhaus* was sounded when the Nazi press labeled the structure "degenerate art." In 1938, with no buyers interested in even bidding, the *Kugelhaus* was demolished.

2005: Dreams occasionally die, and some die harder than others. The *Kugelhaus* memory lay dormant for sixty-five years. One likes to believe that freedom begets creativity, and in Dresden it seems to have been the case. In the Old City at the Wienerplatz stands the first of what eventually will be five *Kugelhaus* examples in the city. Unlike the original *Kugelhaus,* this is not a standalone. Rather it is a commercial building embedded in a more conventional construction. Likewise, in Berlin Mitte—once upon a time East Berlin—a rather more independent-standing *Kugelhaus* beckons retail buyers. Even the idea of a livable family *Kugelhaus* is also out there experimentally. These turn up here and there as well as in popular science and futurist periodicals. For sheer beauty, however, it will be difficult to achieve the nighttime vision of Dresden's original, when *Das Kugelhaus* was lit up from the inside.

And what about the Exhibition grounds and the spot where the great *Kugelhaus* captured so much attention? The Exhibition grounds house the Volkswagen Transparent Factory, where every aspect of auto assembly—most of it by robots—is clearly visible to visitors. A tall cylindrical transparent tower, partially reminiscent of the *Kugelhaus,* occupies the spot of the original. On completion, each auto is automatically sent to the transparent tower, one level of vehicles mounted upon the other. When a buyer arrives to pick up an order, the designated vehicle is plucked automatically

Auto of the future, at the VW Transparent Factory

from the tower and delivered to the entrance of the factory, no doubt with panache. The driver is handed the keys and drives off to places unknown, whether they be in Germany or somewhere in China, these days the main consumer of VW's luxury vehicle, the Phaeton.

THE DRESDEN POSTSCRIPT: Six months before the magic carpet adventure, while plans were being made, each of the travelers seemed to have a special reason for wanting to include Dresden. In the case of the three who had seen Dresden in its troubled times, why not a revisit to the city, now free and without doubt up-and-coming?

Finally, there was Robert, a bona fide enthusiast when it comes to classic automobiles. A few he owns; others he might one day like to own. Dresden? Robert had read about the city's Volkswagen Transparent Factory, where every aspect of auto assembly is visible to visitors. As plans solidified, it was clear Michael was no less tantalized. Weeks before setting out on the adventure, he reserved a tour of the factory—four visitors, English language, 3:00 P.M. on Saturday of the *Wende* weekend. Had Michael specified Finnish or Urdu or Farsi, or some more esoteric language, no doubt the Transparent Factory would still have delivered on time.

By taxi from the Westin Bellevue on the Elbe to the Transparent Factory on the *Kugelhaus* grounds. Then a formal welcome by a bevy of attractive young women and men all dressed in formal black suits and starched white shirts, collars open. Theirs is truly a class act. The visitors surmise this is indeed Volkswagen's intention. Most surprising, yet so appropriate, in the center of the great customer lobby stands a giant sphere, slightly submerged into the floor. It is described in the promotional literature as "a tribute to the world's first '*Kugelhaus*,' which stood here from 1928 to 1938."

When the time comes, the four visitors are escorted to an elevator, rising to the main assembly level above, all set out on polished parquet floors. In honor of this important holiday weekend, the production line is standing still, but nearby stand the assemblers themselves—rather, the masters of the robots—each in an appropriate starched uniform, ready to answer questions in English or German. Even as other groups come off the elevator, no effort is made to hurry along the ever-curious German/English foursome. The final surprise is a glimpse of two futuristic VW passenger vehicles—mockups still on the drawing board. No one is disappointed. In fact, one might imagine one of them standing in the driveway of some futuristic *Kugelhaus* residence.

It should not come as a surprise that Robert, on his return home to Minnesota, promptly placed an order for a new Volkswagen Jetta. This will be the first VW in his growing collection of classic automobiles.

Berlin Beyond the Crossing

14

Mitte

IN THE MIDDLE OF BERLIN: And so it has always been. In those early times, like most cities, Berlin was protected by a wall of fortifications, in other words, a fortified castle. Unlike the Berlin wall of the twentieth century, the role of the castle wall was to keep *out* potential enemies and other strangers. Yet outside the wall, a place of commerce was slowly evolving, beginning with a cattle market. No doubt the market was owned by a Jew. One must believe no Jew was allowed within the fortified walls. Such were the beginnings of Mitte.

The original fortified castle was located on what is now Museum Island in the Spree River. By 1443, the city was bursting with commercial development and the human energy that goes with it—no more cattle markets outside the wall. The ruling Hohenzollern margrave—Friedrich II-Irontooth—thus felt it prudent to move his princely residence from the countryside into the city. From old Iron Tooth's perspective, the Berlin population was getting out of hand, requiring a more visible presence of the margrave's power. From then on the urban expansion, modernization, and beautification went forward in earnest, all to demonstrate the wealth and power resident in the Berlin castle—a palace in the making.

By the nineteenth century, Berlin was in all ways the royal city of Prussia's Hohenzollern kings—their city residence located precisely in the middle of Mitte. When Friedrich Wilhelm III was crowned in 1797, not unlike his ancestor centuries earlier, he declared the morals and ethics of the city to be fraught with decadence. He would rule as a reformer! Eight years into his rule, for whatever reason, he invited Tsar Alexander I of Russia to visit Berlin. No doubt an alliance was in the making, for certainly Alexander was no reformer.

ALEXANDERPLATZ: Across from the royal residence lay a broad area of mixed use. The impact of the great industrial revolution had already had an impact on Frederich Wilhelm's kingdom. Why not honor the visiting Russian by naming that large area across from the royal palace Alexanderplatz—and so it was done. One can imagine that in doing so Friedrich Wilhelm felt a bit of envy. "*Tsar*[37] Alexander?" Why not "Kaiser Friedrich Wilhelm?"

King Friedrich Wilhelm ruled for some forty years. Although his reign included a number of great battles with neighboring kingdoms, it also included as many defeats. By the time of his death in 1840, he had done little to ennoble his realm. Indeed he had become the despot that he earlier despised.

[Sometimes history does repeat itself, sort of. Ninety years later, Adolf Hitler was on the rise, in Berlin. A seat in the Reichstag [Parliament], potentially the chancellorship, ultimately the role of Führer were all in his sights. The candidate's message was multifaceted, but among the issues repeated over and over was the decay of culture in society. He railed against the new art, modern theater, contemporary literature, and even sterile architecture. Worse was the decadence of morals in the nation, especially in the dens of iniq-

---

[37]"Tsar" or "Czar": in German, "Kaiser"; in English, "Emperor."

uity that floated across the capital city of Berlin, principally in Mitte. And of course it was all because of the Jews. Hitler and his party would change all that. One can imagine this message finding resonance in much of the middle class across the nation. And of course it did. Friedrich Wilhelm's unhappy legacy back in 1840 would be dwarfed by that of Adolf Hitler.]

Back now to the nineteenth century and the end of King Friedrich Wilhelm's reign. Enter Otto von Bismarck, who had the ear of the king's son, Wilhelm I of Prussia. Bismarck not only created a modern German Empire but so hastened the industrial revolution in Germany that by 1900 the nation's economy was the largest in Europe. Thus did Otto von Bismarck, master of manipulation as well as diplomacy, create a new German *Reich* [empire], encompassing much of central and western Europe. And thus did King Wilhelm I of Prussia become *Kaiser* Wilhelm I of Germany's Second Reich.

Mitte, the oldest part of Berlin, was attracting immigrants not only from across the new Germany, but also from German holdings in Poland. Presumably good times lay ahead! But it didn't work out quite that way. On the Kaiser's death, his grandson was crowned Kaiser Wilhelm II. Bismarck no longer ran the show. World War I was on the horizon, and in short order it arrived. Over four years, the high cost in young men's lives and the nation's once rich financial standing delivered nothing but defeat and the resignation of the Kaiser, followed by an inglorious treaty signed at Versailles in France. It was a treaty the United States Senate refused to ratify.

15

Weimar

OUT OF THE ASHES, LIKE A PHOENIX: Yes, the Weimar Republic was about to emerge. In the old city of Weimar, a National Assembly was designing a democratic, parliamentary, federal government for the twentieth century. It would be a product of the Enlightenment.[38] Yet the Versailles Treaty that Germany was forced to sign, contained provisions meant to keep that nation weak indefinitely. And who would have predicted the inflation that was about to destroy the German nation at a time when a postwar economic recovery was barely in its infancy? In hindsight, the Weimar Republic was doomed from the beginning.

Yet in Berlin and especially in Mitte, the Bauhaus architectural revolution was born; the iconic film *der Blaue Engel* with Marlene Dietrich was a sensation; George Grosz captured the heady culture in paintings; British poets W.H. Auden and Stephen Spender put the mood to poetry;

---

[38]"The Enlightenment" was, at its broadest, a philosophical movement of the eighteenth century. It stressed human reasoning over blind faith or obedience and encouraged scientific thinking. Beginning in the nineteenth century, its influence affected all European nations one way or another.

120

Bertold Brecht, playwright, and Kurt Weill, composer, together created *The Threepenny Opera;* Carl Jung reinvented psychology; intellectuals roamed the streets and discoursed in the halls of the University of Berlin; Albert Einstein directed the Wilhelm Institute for Physics; political and sociological groupings, from the left to the far left, appeared spontaneously, initially with little room for those on the right.

Yet in southern Germany—Dresden, Leipzig, Munich, and elsewhere—daily marches and sometimes street battles tended to pit the far left against a new far right. In Berlin, however, especially in Mitte, the encounters were mostly among the various forms of Marxism, some within the democratic system, others still bent on a revolution in the spirit of Lenin. Once the Nazi movement went mainstream, these loyalties would be subsumed by fear of the real enemy.

Over at the Reichstag, in spite of political instability, the democratically elected German government was looking ahead. In Berlin, plans were drawn up and generally executed to create a nobler Alexanderplatz with wider thoroughfares to serve the expanding commercial sector in Mitte. Even when in 1929 the Great Depression descended on America, there was still good ferment in Berlin and for sure in Mitte.

But it was all over by January of 1933. After three parliamentary elections within just a few weeks, it became clear that a majority government could not be formed. The Nazi Party[39] came in third with 18.3 percent of the vote. In a desperate compromise, assumed to be but temporary, Adolf Hitler was nevertheless chosen chancellor and three other Nazi Party members given posts in the government. Adolf Hitler was sworn in the evening of January 30. The crowds on all sides of the great Brandenburg Gate were larger than

---

[39]*Nationalsozialistische Deutsche Arbeiterpartei (NSDAP);* in common usage, the Nazi Party.

ever witnessed before, and when the new chancellor finally appeared at a Reichstag window, with spotlights focused on him, pandemonium broke loose. Likewise in other cities of the nation—marching of party members, SA[40] and SS[41] parading in uniform, and street rallies of a people drunk with joy. After that things moved very fast. New elections in February. On the twenty-seventh of the month, fire in the Reichstag, blamed on the Communists, no doubt set by the Nazis. Events moved even faster now. At Hitler's insistence, President Hindenberg suspended civil liberties. On March 5 another election, with the Nazis receiving forty-four percent of the vote and the German National Peoples Party eight percent, together a majority of fifty-two percent.

By now the uniformed party members were everywhere on the street. Already Berlin's Police Department had been taken over by the SS. The several political parties on the left, long imbedded within the Mitte population and beyond, were desperately trying to unify, but it was far too late.

From Victor Klemperer's diary:

January 30, 1933: Hitler becomes chancellor.

March 10: I heard a part of Hitler's speech from Königsberg. The front of a hotel at the railway station, illuminated, a torch-light procession in front of it, torchbearers and swastika-flag bearers on the balconies and loud speakers. I understood only occasional words. But the tone! The unctuous bawling, truly bawling, of a priest.

On March 27, 1933, the enforcement of a new law allowing "ruling by decree." Thus was the transformation of Mitte, Berlin, and all of Germany complete.

---

[40] *Sturm Abteilung,* in English, Protection Corps; also called the Brown Shirts.

[41] *Schutzstafel,* in English, Storm Troopers.

EPITAPH: The Weimar Republic was born in 1919 amid a catastrophe and died in 1933 amid an even greater catastrophe. In the fourteen years of its reign, Weimar challenged all aspects of modern culture—avant-garde at the time, yet today fully at home throughout the western world and much of the east. What a magnificent run and what a legacy left behind.

16

Götterdämmerung[42]

The Nazi takeover of Germany did not diddle: immediately the Communists, then the Jews—little by little, yet with continuing acceleration. In 1936 the remilitarizing of the Rhineland on the west, bringing cheers from the German people, more pressures on the Jews, even more boldness by the government when the "Jewish Problem" elicited so little response from foreign neighbors. So emboldened by this cheap success, in 1938 Germany added Austria to the mix. The military may have feared a fight, but it turned out to be a festival of joy. That summer a conference at Munich, where Hitler asked for just a little piece of Czechoslovakia and promised this would satisfy. France and England said okay. Yet hardly was the ink dry when Germany occupied all of Czechoslovakia—Hitler's first major acquisition. Then three months later—November 9-10—*Kristallnacht* left Jewish communities in shambles and Jews scrambling for exit with little more than the clothes on their backs.

Bigger fish were now in the German government's sights— first of all Poland, the need for *Lebensraum*[43] and all that

[42]Twilight of the gods.

[43]Living space.

nonsense. By a secret protocol, Germany and the Soviet Union agreed to split the Polish landscape. For Germany, there was no longer anything to fear from the east. In September 1939, the German Panzers just rolled through Poland. Hardly three weeks later, with the Soviets completing the squeeze, Polish forces were forced to surrender. Thus began the great massacre of Polish civilians—priests, intellectuals, ordinary folk, and of course always the Jews. German forces now turned west—Belgium, France, the Netherlands, Denmark, Norway. And it had all been so easy, so it seemed. With their nation's successes so extraordinary, even doubting Germans were taken aback. If they questioned the wisdom of these aggressive trends, it was better to remain silent. In Germany opposition could be harshly dealt with.

Only the island kingdom of Britain, badly beaten on the Continent but hanging on at home, was spared. Rather, German forces turned back to the east for the greatest prize of all, the European portion of the Soviet Union. Once again the Panzers rolled, for this was to be the war of the millennium—"Barbarossa" they called it, after the King Friedrich Barbarossa of the twelfth century. Once again this would be a heroic time that would culminate in a heroic victory. In Barbarossa's case, his legacy was meant to be the capture of Jerusalem, but Jerusalem always eluded him. In his last and greatest crusade to the Holy Land, he began with 100,000 warriors and ended up with just 5,000. Yet Jerusalem remained in the hands of Islam.

The modern Barbarossa commenced in June 1941, an ambitious venture from the Baltic to the Black Sea. From the beginning it was fraught with difficulties. The battles became only more bloody, more deadly, as the invaders pressed forward. In the south, the pinnacle to be reached was the capture of Stalingrad,[44] Stalin's namesake city, with a

---

[44]Now back to its historic name Volgograd.

population of 850,000. When it was all over after a half-year of struggle, Stalingrad was almost empty of human life. What was left of the German armies finally surrendered. Such was the turning point of the war on Germany's eastern front and indeed a turning point in World War II. As for Moscow, the German offensive never got beyond the suburbs. And Leningrad?[45] After almost three years of blockade and a million civilian deaths, Hitler's forces turned back from the gates of the city.

Still, it would be another year before the grand Soviet offensive reached heartland Germany and another four months after that until the final Battle for Berlin.

PRINZ ALBRECHT PRISON: Beginning April 20, 1945, like a deck of cards falling headlong into the center of Alexanderplatz, street by street, building by building, German forces were falling back. To say the Soviet forces were superior would be an understatement. This was the day for which they had lived, and died, ever since June of 1941. The barrage began with long-range shelling followed by a million men—and women—to take down this last piece of German power. Their armies had at last encircled Berlin on all sides. Hitler was still issuing orders from his bunker under the Chancery garden. The military must fight to the death, so too Berlin's civilians. Yet onward came the enemy, finally converging at the historic center of German power. Their goal in these waning days of World War II was to reach Hitler's bunker and also to capture the fabled Reichstag building. It didn't matter that since the day of the fire in 1933 the Reichstag had been mostly empty of everything but trash. The Nazis adopted this symbol of better days before the First War to their own propaganda purposes.

However, beginning with the British bombings in 1943, the Reichstag roof was established as a major control center

---

[45]Now back to its historic name St. Petersburg.

and key location for antiaircraft defense. The building had been bombed repeatedly by British and American planes, but there it stood, proudly withstanding the enemy in its own way. Not far away on the Prinz-Albrecht-Strasse stood an SS interrogation center that could better be called a series of torture chambers. One Franz Lange was arrested on April 9, having been identified as a member of a group working to hasten the capitulation. On the twenty-fourth, just five of his seventy to eighty fellow prisoners were still alive, the rest having been killed one way or another.[46] Franz Lange would survive to tell the tale:

> These five are still fixed in my memory: Father August Reinicke, accused of participating in the July 20[47] episode by harboring a refugee overnight; a German non-commissioned officer who had been caught operating a radio behind the German front line on behalf of the Red Army; a Polish prisoner who had refused to join the German army; a prisoner from Alsace who likewise had refused; and Major Buttler, who had been taken into "protective" custody after his father, the commanding general in Königsberg,[48] had dared to capitulate.

> *May 1, 1945:* The fighting was upon us and the direct bombardment of Prinz-Albrecht-Strasse began. The walls of the cellar were blown open. We all were led through a secret door into another locked space. The prisoner who had operated a radio on behalf of the Red Army was shot. We discussed the possibility of overwhelming our SS guards if indeed they intended to kill us all. They were trembling with fear for they had too much blood on their hands and the Red Army was coming ever nearer. We remaining five lay flat on the ground

[46]Sandvoss, Hans-Rainer, *Widerstand in Mitte und Tiergarten 1933-1945,* pp. 383-4; see Bibliography.

[47]July 20, 1944, the failed attempt involving high-ranking German military officers and civilians in a plot to assassinate Hitler. The place: Hitler's command post in East Prussia.

[48]Since 1945, Kaliningrad in Russia.

and hardly spoke, each of us deep in his own thoughts. Major Buttler had already declared he would never fight against a German soldier. To me it was clear that our freedom could only happen through the Red Army. Father Reinicke began to pray aloud, instilling in each of us the will to stay alive. It was a prayer I shall never forget even though I had never entered a church since my 16th birthday! Toward afternoon the noise in the building complex increased. Our SS captors led us to a space outside the cell, then slipped out in a group. We prisoners were left behind. We waited through the evening and the entire night.

Early in the morning, German General Helmuth Weidling surrendered Berlin to Soviet General Chuikov. Afterward Father Reinicke[49] wrote:

May 2: Close to six o'clock in the morning we heard the shouting of the Russians. The Red Army had come into the building. Their steps came nearer. We pounded against the doors. The window shutters were opened from the outside and a Russian was yelling at us. My answer, in Russian: "We are prisoners." A few minutes later an axe smashed the wood and the door flew open. I was standing face to face opposite a young Red Army female soldier. We were free!

The soldiers were laughing, they slapped us on the shoulder, gave us cigarettes. *"Krieg aus, Hitler kaputt, Goebbels vergiftet."*[50] So they cried to us. Then they sent us to a kitchen to furnish us with provisions for our way home. Outside a scene of horror greeted me: the shot-up park, the bombed out city, the field covered with bodies of human beings and horses, the war material of the Russians—tools of their overwhelming rage— first steps to bring about order, and young female Russian soldiers using flags to direct traffic.

[49]Sandvoss, Hans-Rainer, *Widerstand in Mitte und Tiergarten 1933-1945,* pp. 383-4; see Bibliography.

[50]In English, "War finished, Hitler broken, Goebbels poisoned."

The cost in lives from the Berlin battle is estimated at 125,000 civilian deaths, 50,000 German military deaths, and 81,000 Soviet deaths. Actually, no one knows exactly.

Berlin was eighty percent destroyed, Mitte closer to ninety percent destroyed, and the Alexanderplatz neighborhood virtually one hundred percent destroyed. And in a way, historically, the Russians won the prize. Ruins of the most historic buildings, representing the glory days of Prussia and the Second German Reich, found themselves within the Soviet sector of Berlin. Only the Reichstag stood outside, in the American-occupied sector. At first, location didn't make that much difference, but after 1961, when the Berlin Wall sealed off East Berlin from West Berlin, hence from the rest of the free world, the Reichstag was little more than a historical curiosity. In fact, the Berlin wall ran directly behind the building.

17

Postscript to the Twentieth Century

A merican tourists from a time now past:

December 1956: Jane, much later of the Volvo foursome, with husband and two-year-old daughter Ilse, were visiting Ilse's German grandmother in Berlin. West Berlin was still in recovery mode; however, what was new were several modern office buildings, each well lit with the name of the owner—in every case a German insurance company. One must presume in 1956 here was where the money lay. The American family spent a day with friends Sigurd Sigurdsen and his wife. Sigurd was a Norwegian diplomat who for a time had been stationed in Jane's home city. Now he was a member of the Norwegian military presence in this still-occupied city.

Riding in an official auto with a tiny Norwegian flag flying on its fender, the American visitors were whisked through security at the Brandenburg Gate, thus entering East Berlin along *Unter den Linden*. This was once the grand avenue of an earlier Berlin. Yet in 1956 there was barely a single person nor an automobile on the wide, parklike avenue nor a single Linden tree. In the last year of the war and the first year after the war. Berlin's fabled parkland and forests of yore had been totally cut down by the population. In those two years there was virtually no fuel while winter temperatures sank to historic lows. On the other hand, both sides of the parkway were occupied by new, taller buildings, some even bombastic. The visitors understood these were retail stores, but nobody appeared to be buying. They were told the shelves were empty. Food and other products in short supply. At each visible street crossing, the visitors could peer behind the buildings—nothing, just blocks and blocks of emptiness. Obviously the massive rubble had been hauled away somewhere. All Jane could think of were Russian Empress Catherine's Potemkin Villages.[51]

May 1973: Jane was on her way from Dresden to Berlin by train and alone. Days before, she had entered East Germany by train, coming from Frankfurt. With a proper East Germany Dresden hotel reservation made earlier from home, as required, and expecting to make her own hotel reservation once she reached West Berlin, Jane had confidently boarded the train for the short daytime journey. But on reaching the East Berlin station, she was pulled into Security and relieved of her passport, no explanation, later questions about why she entered from the west and now wanted to leave East Germany from a point far to the north. Didn't she know one must leave East Germany from the point at which one entered East Germany? No, she did not. No one had told her. Again left alone, but eventually reunited with her passport.

Quite intimidated by then, Jane boarded the electric streetcar *(S-Bahn)*. Her destination point was the Visitor's Bureau in West Berlin, just beyond the Soviet sector. The streetcar had not traveled far before it stopped unexpectedly. Two men in uniform boarded and went directly to a well-dressed man with a briefcase several seats in front of the visitor. What was said, Jane did not hear. The man stood up and left with the two uniformed men, each holding firmly to one of his arms. Jane fol-

---

[51]As the story goes, one Grigory Potemkin, back in 1787 minister to Russian Empress Catherine the Great, had fake facades of villages constructed along the banks of the Dnieper River in the Crimea prior to the Empress's visit. Having led the Crimean military campaign, he wanted to impress her as to the value of her new conquests. These days the tale is considered a myth.

lowed the drama with her eyes, noting that not one of the other passengers dared watch. They kept their eyes averted, heads bent down.

On November 4, 1989, a million people gathered on Alexanderplatz to demonstrate against their East German government. It was the largest antigovernment demonstration in history. Five days later the Berlin Wall was breached. That was when everything changed.

18

Berlin in the Twenty-first Century

Today, as the magic carpet is rolling into Berlin, history doesn't even seem to matter. Everything is up-to-date, if not already pushing the curve. The Volvo crowd, foremost Michael, is already impatient to meet up with his sister, Katrina Söderberg-Jahn. She is a dear friend to Jane and Helen from their 1999 mission to Pomerania. The travelers are also eager to discover what is new in this ever-changing metropolis. Over the cell phone they learn Katrina is already sitting in the lounge of the Park Inn Hotel, a grand piece of the Radisson hotel empire. They remember the hotel from earlier times when it was the Forum Hotel, if not grand at least exceedingly pleasant.

But still they make a stop along the way, for the flea market bug has not yet been satisfied. Either by accident or by purpose, the magic Volvo has found its way to the current "in" district of East Berlin. It is Boxhagenerplatz in the Friedrichshain section of the city, an entire block with paved walks and well-organized shops—Sunday only. The four visitors scatter in all directions. Jane is on her way to a book stall, perhaps a book on the *Frauenkirche,* the most recently completed Dresden landmark, where Michael and Helen attended a Bach concert a night ago. Helen is off some-

133

Success at the Boxhagenerplatz flea market

Katrina Söderberg-Jahn, with Helen, at the Park Inn Hotel

where, seeking out unique drawer-pulls for a favorite chest at home. Their male companions are elsewhere, somewhere. Jane has success in a stall with beautiful books of art and architecture. Miraculously, an exquisite book about Dresden's *Frauenkirche,* so recently resurrected, is among them. Flushed with success, she finds Helen still at the drawer-pull stall where she has just finished purchasing her chosen drawer-pulls. Jane turns over to her friend the precious book. It will be a birthday gift from Helen to her brother, who earlier had visited Dresden when the historic *Frauenkirche* was not yet open. How it happens, one cannot say. Even without GPS, Helen and Jane and Robert and Michael all meet up with each other at the same time on the same corner from which they entered the flea market.

As for the drawer-pulls, Helen will later discover they don't exactly fit. She can't open the drawers, but the pulls certainly do look pretty on the bureau. She will leave them there. And the *Frauenkirche* book? Her brother will receive it on his birthday. He will be mighty pleased to see the extraordinary pictures, even without an English text. Both brother and sister agree: Everything can't be perfect.

THE REUNION: Katrina spots the new arrivals just as they round one of the large pillars. She stands and returns a few embraces while receiving eager handshakes, all as appropriate. She has just arrived by train from a hospital in Cologne, where a dear friend is not expected to live much longer. Nevertheless she stands with all the dignity and simple elegance of a royal highness—at least in Jane's imagination. Katrina and Michael are of course the great grandchildren of Ruth von Kleist of Kieckow, now known in the literature as the *Matriarch of Conspiracy.* Katrina conveys her immense joy at the long-planned reunion, pleasure in knowing about the combined adventures thus far, and high expectations for the morrow. Someone would have to look deeply into her pale blue eyes to find the tinge of sadness from knowing that her dear friend cannot be with us and is indeed failing fast.

The Park Inn is a sight to behold—mostly in white with check-in counter, bar, restaurant, and lounge all seeming to flow smoothly from one to the other, all at street level and well connected to indoor parking and tour-bus stops, likewise well-organized to deal with *Die Wende* weekend crowd. They come by auto, by taxi, by train, by tourist bus, all to celebrate the change that occurred back on October 3, 1990. That was the day East German representatives at the Palace of the Republic in East Berlin and BDR representatives at the West German Capital in Bonn simultaneously signed documents reuniting Germany under the banner BRD— *Bund der Republik Deutschland.* Then as an afterthought— though perhaps the most important decision of all—the reunited nation's capital to be once more at home in Berlin.

The room check-in completed, it is time the final five should gather for a glass of wine and an early supper. Today, October 2, is Helen's birthday, the second of the two birthdays celebrated within the week, both of which were also celebrated some years ago on a similar occasion in Szczecin, Poland. Once more the travelers are on an exploratory journey they only now begin to comprehend, even as the journey is drawing to a close.

TOURISTS ON THE LOOSE All in a single day, on foot. Begin with the boat ride on the Spree River, as if that great river, now narrowed to a width of some fifty meters, has been following the foursome all the way from the Saxon Fish Trap with its soft sausage.[52] Quite a different environment. On the west bank, the national library with the glass-covered memorial to two thousand "degenerate" books destroyed in a once-celebrated Nazi burning on the same spot. One can look down through the transparent glass cover and view under-

[52]See page 46.

ground replicas of all two thousand books lined up on wooden shelves beneath the surface. Then behind the library the transparent dome of the reborn Reichstag, on which tourists can circle inside and look down through the clear glass ceiling to observe the workings of the German Parliament. On the west bank also the new ultra-modern Chancery, with the German flag fluttering on the flagpole. This, they are told, means Chancellor Angela Merkel is working in her office today. On the east bank of the river stands a row of modest buildings that formerly housed the armed Berlin Wall guards. The wall was on the west bank. The river was the death strip. Over twenty-eight years, some two hundred and fifty people were killed trying to escape through the wall, including attempts to swim across the Spree River either on the surface or under the water. That was until the East Berlin guards lowered the water level to prevent such foolishness. These revelations have sobered the visitors as they return to the boat landing for disembarkation.

Back on shore, they walk to the nearby Marx-Engels Forum, a large open park with a pair of very large and unlikely bronze sculptures. These are stylized depictions of Karl Marx sitting on a box and Friedrich Engels, his co-author of the 1848 *Communist Manifesto,* standing to his left. Among the five tourists, it is Jane with whom the two bronzes seem to resonate most. They do appear to be such pleasant and harmless fellows. How can one not like them? Yet after the Berlin Wall came down, there was great pressure to remove the sculptures and rename the entire park. To its detractors it represented some of the worst of Berlin history. Meanwhile times have changed. Karl and Friedrich still survive. In fact they are now a favorite tourist attraction.

Still in Mitte, and not far from Alexanderplatz, the quintet of visitors marches on to the Nikolai Quarter. First and foremost to visit the Church of St. Nicholas, the oldest church in Berlin. It stands near where the cattle market once reigned just outside the city walls. Parts of the church date from the

The Reichstag Transparent Dome, from the Spree River

Calling on Karl Marx and Friedrich Engels

year 1200. Its two towers from medieval times were destroyed in World War II bombings. It took some time, but in 1981 the East German government restored the church and rebuilt its distinctive towers using the original plans. Katrina reminds her American friends that in the seventeenth century, Germany's greatest composer of Christian hymns was pastor of the St. Nicholas Church—his name, Paul Gerhardt. Later back home Jane will research this German of whom Katrina speaks so highly. She will contact Dr. Philip Brunelle,[53] the music director of her church. Philip's reply:

> Paul Gerhardt, 1607-1676, grew up during the Thirty Years" War. He became the favorite pastor and preacher at St. Nicholas Church in Berlin. All through those years he was also writing poetry and hymns, even as he lost four of his five children to the Plague. Altogether he wrote 133 hymns. These are considered among the greatest works of art in the German language. There are no other German writers whose hymns have found their way into the English language as have those of this modest pastor. Paul Gerhardt is said to be the greatest writer of Christian hymns since the Reformation. At Plymouth Church on Good Friday we sing "O Sacred Head, Now Wounded." We also sing "All My Heart Rejoices," "Come, Your Hearts and Voices Raising," and "Awake, My Heart, with Gladness." This last hymn we sang this year on Easter.

[53]Dr. Philip Brunelle, director of music at Plymouth Congregational Church in Minneapolis, is recognized locally and nationally for the breadth of his sacred and other music choices—old and new, as well as esoteric—choral and otherwise. Plymouth Church is also known for its choir and congregational hymn singing. The improvisations with which Dr. Brunelle introduces the hymns provide weekly inspiration for members and visitors alike. He has received a multitude of national and international awards, including the Kodaly Medal from the government of Hungary, the Royal Order of the Polar Star from the King of Sweden, Honorary Member of the Order of the British Empire and Commander of the Royal Norwegian Order of Merit. And that is just the beginning.

Keeping pace with Dresden's transparent VW assembly plant and the
Reichstag's transparent dome, the Park Inn guest rooms now have
transparent baths.

In 2000, Katrina and Jane together visited the church and
had lunch at a sidewalk café nearby. At that time it seemed
no longer to be a church, but rather a museum with a bulletin board of activities for the neighborhood youth.
Nowadays the St. Nicholas church occasionally holds religious services, no doubt with the singing of hymns by Paul
Gerhardt. On this last day together in Berlin, the touring
quintet finds the church still to be a museum with a bulletin
board of activities for the neighborhood youth. And a mixed
neighborhood it is. The Nikolai Quarter lies in the center of
Mitte, and Mitte, with a population of 328,000, lies in the
center of Berlin. Within Mitte, 55.5 percent are Ethnic
Germans and 45.5 percent are from other nations:
Muslim/Middle Eastern origin, 60,000; non-German
European origin, 35,000; East Asians, sub-Saharan Africans,
etc., 48,000. To Jane it sounds like New York City in the first
decades of the twentieth century.

Time for an afternoon snack at a sidewalk café nearby.

AUF WIEDERSEHEN: The last evening of the journey is difficult for the Americans. So dependent have they been on patient, good-natured, and knowledgeable Michael—and now barely time enough to put their feelings properly into words; so little time to reminisce on earlier adventures with Katrina, nor to recollect the extraordinary life of her (and Michael's) mother Raba.[54] Such is the last evening in the Park Inn at Alexanderplatz.

Early in the morning, off to the familiar Tegel Airport. The three Americans board a waiting taxi while Katrina and Michael stand by to bid adieu. Katrina will return by train to her friend's hospital bed in Cologne and Michael will drive his magic Volvo back home to Heidelberg and to Gun, his bride of many years.

And the future? Yes, they vow to meet again, but where? Koszalin, Berlin, Gdańsk, Dresden, Stuttgart, possibly Warsaw? The Lord willing, it will be somewhere in this mortal world.

---

[54]Söderberg-Jahn, Katrina, *Rabas Geschichte, Ruth Roberta Ripke-Heckscher, geb. 1909-1997;* see Bibliography.

Epilogue

I met a traveler from an antique land
Who said: Two vast and trunkless legs of stone
Stand in the desert. Near them, on the sand,
Half sunk, a shattered visage lies, whose frown,
And wrinkled lip, and sneer of cold command,
Tell that its sculptor well those passions read
Which yet survive, stamped on these lifeless things,
The hand that mocked them, and the heart that fed;
And on the pedestal these words appear:
"My name is Ozymandias, king of kings;
Look on my works, ye Mighty, and despair!"
Nothing beside remains. Round the decay
Of that colossal wreck, boundless and bare
The lone and level sands stretch far away.

Ozymandias,
Percy Bysshe Shelley
(1792-1822)

Bibliography

Bismarck, Ruth-Alice von and Itz, Ulrich, *Love Letters from Cell 92: The Correspondence Between Dietrich Bonhoeffer and Maria von Wedemeyer, 1943-45.* Nashville, TN: Abingdon Press, 1995.

Brent, Leslie Baruch, *Sunday's Child? A Memoir.* New Romney, UK: Bank House Books, 2009.

Gründig, Claudia, *Dresden, Früher und Heute* [Then and Now]. Köln, Germany: Komet Verlag GmbH, 2009.

Klemperer, Victor, *I Will Bear Witness 1933-1941.* New York: The Modern Library, 1999.

Klemperer, Victor, *I will Bear Witness 1942-1945.* New York: The Modern Library, 2001.

Pacholski, Zdzisław, *Koszalin, 1901–2000.* Koszalin, Poland: Wydawnicza Millennium, 2000.

Pejsa, Jane, *Matriarch of Conspiracy, Ruth von Kleist 1867–1945.* Minneapolis, MN: Kenwood Publishing, 1991.

Pejsa, Jane, *Mission to Pomerania, Where Bonhoeffer Met the Holocaust.* Minneapolis, MN: Kenwood Publishing, 2000.

Pejsa, Jane, *A Remarkable Journey into the Heart of Europe.* Minneapolis, MN: Kenwood Publishing, 2008.

Romanik, Ks. Henryk, *O Żydach W Koszalinie* [About the Jews of Köslin]. Koszalin, Poland: Wydawca Per Media S.A, 2006.

Söderberg-Jahn, Katrina, *Rabas Geschichte* [Raba's Story], *Ruth Roberta Ripke-Heckscher, geb. Stahlberg, 1909-1997.* Hannover, Germany: Privately published, 2002.

Sandvoss, Hans-Rainer, *Widerstand 1933-1945* [Resistance]. Berlin: Gedenkstätte Deutscher Widerstand, 1994.

Temme, J.D.H., *Volkssagen von Pommern und Rügen* [Collected Folktales]. Berlin: Nikolaischen Buchhandlung, 1840.

Vonnegut, Kurt, *Slaughterhouse-Five.* New York: Dial Press, a Division of Random House, 1997.

Zimmerling, Peter, *Starke fromme Frauen* [Strong Religious Women]. Giessen, Switzerland: Brunnen Verlag, 1996.

Index of Names

Auden, W.H., 120
Augustus I, Prince of Saxony, 100-103, 106, 109-110
Augustus II, King of Poland, 100-103, 106, 109-110
Augustus II, Prince of Saxony, 101, 104
Augustus III, King of Poland, 101, 104
Bach, Johann Sebastian, 107
Barbarossa, King Friedrich, 125
Bender, Stephen, 125
Bismarck, Otto von, 119
Bleicker, Joachim, 44-45
Bonhoeffer, Dietrich, 7, 15-18
Bottger, Johann, 109-110
Brecht, Berthold, 121
Brent, Leslie Baruch, 37-41
Brunelle, Philip, 139
Buttler, Major, 127
Chuikov, General Vasily, 128
Churchill, Winston, 74, 81-85
Clay, General Lucius, 88
Dietrich, Marlene, 120
Einstein, Albert, 121
Empress Catherine of Russia, 131
Engels, Friedrich, 137, 138
Gerhardt, Paul, 139
Goebbels, Josef, 128
Gorbachev, Mikhail, 96
Hauptmann, Marianne and family, 92-95

Hindenburg, President Paul von, 122
Hitler, Adolf, 14, 56-128 passim
Hohenzollern, Friedrich Wlhelm III, 118
Hohenzollern, Kaiser Wilhelm I and II, 119
Honecker, Erik, 96
Hüneke, Martin, 97
Kästner, Erich, 99
Kennedy, John F., 88
Kleist of Kieckow, Family von, 11-25
Kleist-Klein Krössin, Ruth von, 11-18
Kleist-Schmenzin, Ewald von, 14
Klemperer diary excerpts, 55-75, 122
Klemperer, Victor and Eva, 51-77 passim, 101
Klimt, Gustav, 6
Kuehn, Aunt Helen, 99
Kuehn, Helen, 6-141 passim
Lange, Franz, 127
Luther, Martin, 102, 106-107
Marshall, General George, 86
Marx, Karl, 76, 137-138
Merkel, Chancellor Angela, 138
Mussolini, Benito, 103
Ozymandias, King of Kings, 143
Pabst, Friedrich, Hitler's architect, 103

Pacholski, Zdzisław (Zibi), 32-46
  passim
Parsons, Marie Volkert, 7
Pejsa, Jane, 6-141 passim
Potemkin, Grigory, 131
Reinicke, Father August, 128
Ripke Söderberg-Jahn, Katrina,
  21, 89-90, 107-141
Ripke, Michael, 5-141 passim
Ripke-Heckscher, Raba and fam-
  ily, 89-90, 141
Romanik, Ks. Henryk, 32-46
Romanov, Anastasia, 12-13
Romanov, Tsar Alexander I, 118
Romanov, Tsar Nicholas, 12, 83
Romeyko, Radek and Grażyna,
  20-25

Rommel, General Erwin, 81
Roosevelt, Franklin D., 74, 81-84
Rousseau, Jean, 77
Rühlow, Gerhard, 8-10
Scheller, Rita, 31
Siemon-Netto, Uwe, 87
Sigurdsen, Sigurd, 130
Stalin, Josef, 74, 81-83, 125
Strauss, Richard, 105
Ulbricht, Walter, 87-88
Vockrodt, Robert, 6-141 passim
Voltaire, Francois, 77
Wagner, Richard, 105
Wedemeyer, Marie von, 15-18
Weidling, General Helmuth, 128
Weill, Kurt, 105, 121
Zimmermann, Peter, 20, 21, 23

About the Author

Over the last thirty years, Jane Pejsa has devoted her writing interests to nonfiction. Her first book, *The Molineux Affair,* was a finalist for the 1983 true-crime Edgar Award. A decade later her major work chronicled the martyred Dietrich Bonhoeffer and the brave families that conspired to bring down Hitler and the Nazi regime. Thus was born *Matriarch of Conspiracy,* which has garnered two major awards—the 1992 Minnesota Book Award and the 1992 Independent Publishers Award—now also in Japanese, German, and Polish. Ms. Pejsa received an Alumni Achievement Award from Carleton College and the Golden ex-Libris Award from the Polish State Library in Pomorze.

Following were two biographies of Minnesota women, namely, the librarian Gratia Countryman and a voice from the Ojibwe Emily Peake; also the tale of Michael *Romanoff, Prince of Rogues,* a charming fraud who for two decades tantalized the Hollywood crowd. Both the Romanoff and Gratia Countryman biographies were finalists for a Minnesota Book Award. In *The Final Encounter—Rommel, Patton, Zhukov,* Ms. Pejsa brought three WWII giants together in an antechamber to the Hereafter.

In *Away, Tangled Past,* Jane Pejsa has returned to two countries once caught in a deadly struggle that simply won't leave her mind and heart—Poland and Germany. Her several books in the bibliography have addressed the twentieth-century aspects of this trauma. In this latest book, Ms. Pejsa leads the reader on a journey through Poland on the Baltic, Dresden in Germany, and finally Berlin, out of the ashes of history to discover a culture of community spanning the Oder and Neisse rivers.

Jane and Arthur Pejsa are at home in Minneapolis, Minnesota.